CW00447575

Peaks and Troughs

A Season of Derbyshire Football

by

Paul Hudson

© 2004 Paul Hudson
Castle Heritage Publishing
117A Kedleston Road
Derby
DE22 1FS

Email: admin@castle-heritage.co.uk

ISBN 0 9548509 0 4

Printed by
MOORLEY'S Print & Publishing
23 Park Rd., Ilkeston, Derbys DE7 5DA
Tel/Fax: (0115) 932 0643

Contents

Acknowledgements

Much of the information in the book came from the many websites run by individual football clubs and their fans. Also of note were more general websites including the Football Club History Database www.fchd.btinternet.co.uk and the NCEL website www.ncel.freeserve.co.uk.

Various books were also incredibly useful, especially
A. Rippon, *Derbyshire Football: the first 100 years*,
Derby: Breedon Books, 1983

Also useful were
G. Bannister, An *Official History of Chesterfield Football Club 1866-1991*, Worksop: Ratcliff & Roper, 1991
A. Cope, *A History of Alfreton Town Football Club Vol.1*,
The author, 1998
A. Cope, *A History of Alfreton Town Football Club Vol.2*,
The author, 1999
D. Hale, *Down Wembley Way*, The author, 2000
[about Matlock Town FC]
D. Parkin & J. Fearn, *The Baseball Ground 1895-1997*,
Derby County FC, 1997
D. Payne, *Ilkeston Town: From Hembery to Harbottle*,
ITFC, 1996
A. Rippon & A. Ward, *The Derby County Story*,
Derby: Breedon Books, 1998

Thanks go to the many supporters I met at grounds around the county, and willingly (I hope) talked to this stranger. Also to people who replied to various posts on internet message boards.

Introduction

The idea for this book came a soon after I arrived in Derby. A booklet on Riber Castle had been given to Derby Local Studies Library and Mike, my boss, and I were glancing through it. What caught our eye was not anything to do with the animal park, castle or the house, but the football ground in the distance. Who played there? For two football fanatics, myself with Middlesbrough and Mike with Rangers and Fulham this was an important question.

We got talking about football grounds and a book that had just been written listing every cricket ground in Nottinghamshire. Wouldn't it be an interesting project to discover and visit every football ground in Derbyshire? Duncan Payne, Ilkeston Town and Derbyshire Senior Cup historian was in the library at the time and as we discussed local sides he said that little had been written on local football.

Over the next few months local football news seemed to jump out at me. Just who were the big teams, the teams with history, and the grounds that were out of the ordinary? Intrigued I decided to do something. Harry Pearson's book on North East football, A Far Corner, was one of my favourite books so I decided to spend a season visiting Derbyshire football grounds.

Certain teams or matches were essential as I set out to try and plan out my visits. Derby County features more than once for a number of reasons not least of which being their size compared to other teams. Certain opponents dictated certain games, such as Matlock v Bishop Auckland, and I decided to visit clubs in the High Peak in the spring to avoid the mythical snowdrifts. Others such as Ashbourne Royal Shrovetide Football were tenuous but it was my project and I could choose where to visit.

When I told people about what I was doing they were usually taken aback. "Why do you want to do that?" they asked. Football supporters were often more understanding. Others asked me if I had anything better to do, to which I responded: What is better than this? Actually to be honest there was something I would rather have done but it didn't happen so this was a welcome second choice. It also gave me a wonderful excuse to explore my new home county.

On more than one occasion people looked strangely at me as I scribbled down notes. At Borrowash I had to explain what I was doing a few times. One man looked at me funnily, and asked a friend if he thought I was a scout from another team. "Oh, yes, Real Madrid are sending scouts to see who they should sign", he was told to a chorus of laughs. Ah, perhaps I had missed a trick and could have pretended to be a spy, although whether anyone would have believed me would have been a different matter.

Why Peaks and Troughs? Well apart from a local pun it also sums up football. One season you might be challenging for promotion, the next you could be battling relegation. You may be climbing the pyramid; or else you may be sliding down the leagues. The wonder of individual matches is that you never know what will happen. It all goes to make up the game we love.

I had better apologise in advance for the numerous references to a certain club close to my heart. Twenty years of supporting them will obviously affect me, and what I saw had to compare to this experience. If you think there are a lot of tenuous references I'm afraid you should have seen the ones I left out.

PS The football ground seen from Riber Castle I discovered was Matlock Town's Causeway Lane.

Alfreton Town v Farsley Celtic
North Street
Unibond (Northern Premier League) Division 1
Saturday 17 August 2002

There is something about the first day of the season. There is an anticipation and excitement that has built up week by week without football. After scraps of information about possible signings, departures and friendlies everything bursts into life. Optimism is sky high because you haven't lost yet and you have yet to discover that your latest signing has come from Redcar beach and eats carrots. You know that it is possible for any team, yes even yours, to be top of their table by 4:45. Match and Shoot would have special issues in which I would catch up on news and see the new kits and get the league ladders for the season.

Although a lot of the excitement is still there it does not quite feel the same today. Perhaps it is due to a World Cup during the close season that only seemed to have ended last week, or the blanket coverage in newspapers and club websites providing detailed reports on even reserve friendlies. This season was staggered, with the Scottish Leagues starting one week, the Football League the next, and Premier and non-league clubs the week after. However it was still a start of the season and I was looking forward to it.

At Alfreton they were looking forward to it too. Having won the Northern Counties East League they were now back in the Northern Premier League first division. Alfreton is a medium sized town on the eastern side of the county. An important fact to know should you ever go there is that it is pronounced Olfreton, the first syllable rhyming with the first syllable of Oliver. I learnt this in the first few days at university, after meeting my friend Tim, an Alfreton resident. A small matter maybe but perfectly understandable to someone like myself who prides themselves on parochialism.

Alfreton Town FC is relatively new, having been formed in 1959 from an amalgamation of Alfreton Miners Welfare and Alfreton United. Versions of Alfreton Town had existed from the 19th century onwards, but kept folding and reforming. This incarnation seem to have been fairly steady, staying in the Midlands Counties League for 20 years, and having been in the NPL first division for 11 out of the last 16 seasons.

Success came sporadically with occasional titles, league cups and county cups. The 1973/74 season saw them collect 3 trophies, a feat that they had just repeated. That team featured Mick Wadsworth, current manager of Huddersfield Town having previously managed or coached half a dozen lower league clubs. They won the Midland League Cup three times in a row and were allowed to keep it permanently as a reward.

In the FA Cup, an important feature of non-league football, they had just reached the first round twice. The first time drawing Barrow, then a league club. In this epic tie it took 4 matches, two at neutral venues, before Barrow finally won. They qualified again a few years later but drew another non-league club, Blyth Spartans.

I was pleasantly surprised when I entered the ground at North Street with Tim. It looked a decent ground for this level, and a lot of effort had been spent with most surfaces painted in the bright red club colours. Although not the biggest Reds supporter around Tim had decided to come with me to ensure I was shouting for the right team! The sun was beating down and for possibly the first time in my football attending life, I was wondering if I would regret not wearing sun cream.

Alfreton had had an interesting pre-season like so many other clubs, with many comings and goings. They had unexpectedly had to find a new manager after Chris

Wilder had left to manage Halifax Town. The new boss, David Lloyd (no, not the former tennis player) had signed a number of players including four direct from league clubs. His programme notes were probably a rehash of every other in the country that day, as he expressed his confidence that this squad was capable of doing really well and looked forward to the coming nine months etc. etc.

The match began slowly and was bitty. Neither side could get into a rhythm as passes went out or to the opposition goalkeepers. Ryan France looked good on the right wing, causing Farsley a few problems, although the final ball never seemed to come. Mick Godber also impressed in attack, working hard and managing to get goalside of the defenders on a couple of occasions, but neither time could he beat the goalie. He had scored over 30 goals in the past couple of seasons and watching him today it was easy to believe. Last season he had hit it off with his strike partner Mick Goddard, who scored 32 goals himself, but today was on the subs bench. Strike duos always seem to be better if their names connect. Just think back to Bright and Wright, still together 12 years later with their own radio series, and Shearer and Sutton – SAS.

A minute before half time the match spring into life. France went on a dangerous run but was fouled by Farsley's left winger. Tempers flared as players squared up to each other before the Farsley player was yellow carded. Farsley then failed to clear the free kick as it rebounded around the penalty area. Eventually it came to skipper Darren Brookes on the left-hand side of the area, who blasted it into the net.

At half time I glanced around and tried to estimate the crowd. Wayne Bradley, Alfreton's chairman had called on the people of Alfreton to come and show support, and said he would be disappointed with any crowd below 400, but today it looked below that. It turned out to be 143 less. It is hard to imagine the era when clubs like Alfreton attracted large crowds. Soon after they had reformed they were getting 4 figure crowds and even packed in 5,000 for a local derby with Matlock. Perhaps drawing a Premiership club in the FA Cup might draw that kind of support today, but Unibond league action had not gripped many people's imaginations.

Bradley seemed to be ambitious for the club, and was calling for the support to move the club forward instead of just surviving. They were overseeing an Academy of football for 16-19 year olds, a community coaching programme reaching 1600 children a year, and a link with Sheffield University. Obviously this was not cheap but hopefully they will find the way to continue with this community involvement.

The second half began better than the first half, with Alfreton forcing free kicks, corners and attacks, although few came to anything. Farsley's attacks were handled well by Brookes and Steve Heath, and when they did get shots at goal Stuart Ford, just signed from Ilkeston Town, saved well.

The middle part of the half (if that makes sense) reverted to being scrappy. Tim thought it was because Alfreton were poor and that this was typical non-league football. I wasn't so sure, having witnessed some extremely poor Premier League matches. Perhaps it was because it was a new season and people hadn't settled in yet. Or it could have been the heat. Alternatively it could be just one of those things, when things don't seem to click on the day.

Fortunately Alfreton seemed to get things together towards the end, and managed to get a second goal. Left winger Dolby ran into open space in the Farsley half, and centred it to Godber who turned and scored from the edge of the box. This gave the home side the confidence to attack more and they could have got a third from a late free kick. However it ended 2-0, which was still three points and winning start to their return to the Northern Premier League.

10

I now felt back into the routine, especially when I got home and spent ages pouring over the results on teletext and then watched Match of the Day (or whatever ITV call it) at 10:30. The season had begun.

Alfreton 2-0 Farsley Celtic
Brookes 45, Godber 85

Alfreton: Ford, Bradshaw, Jules, Brookes, Heath, Knapper (Circuit 80), France, Johnson, Godber, Robshaw (Goddard 65), Dolby (Highfield 77).

Farsley: Sutcliffe, Place, Ball, Stabb, Bairstow, Holmes, Smithard, Gray (Watson 60), Henderson (Turner 82), Newton, Beech (Spence 48)

Att: 257

Derby County Reserves v Watford Reserves
Baseball Ground
FA Barclaycard Premier Reserve League (South)
Tuesday 20th August 2002

This was the final match at the Baseball Ground, the end of an era. I must admit that when I came to Derby a year earlier I had presumed that it had already gone since Pride Park had been up 4 years or so. I think many Derby fans were under similar illusions since there was no announcement in the local media or on the club's website about the significance of the game. When I asked in the club shop to check the details I was originally told that there would be a number of matches played there this season and that the game was on Wednesday. I suppose the number of farewells already given can excuse some of this. The last cup match, the last league match, the last last match etc. etc.

Unfortunately I was going to have to miss the opening few minutes of the match because it kicked off at 7:00 and I finished work at 7:00. I hate being late for the start of things; it is a character flaw that most people don't understand. If an invitation says a party starts at 8pm then 8pm is when I arrive and expect it to begin. I have this dread that I have missed something important. At football and cricket I want to soak in the atmosphere, get a programme; listen to the tannoy to check the teams.

I didn't think I would make it at all because for some strange inexplicable reason there were no taxis in the Market Place. Where on earth were they? Then one did arrive and we were off. Have you ever noticed that short cuts are rarely short cuts? They either rely on complicated local knowledge causing non-locals to spend twice as long as they take wrong turnings, or are almost as complicated but take the same amount of time despite being told that it would certainly save you five minutes or more. I had this feeling as the taxi driver first appeared to head towards Pride Park, then swung down various side roads, and just as I was about to ask him what he was doing we had arrived. Obviously the benefit of having 'the knowledge'.

The Baseball Ground was not the original home of Derby County and even after moving there the club didn't even own it for many years. Having being formed by Derbyshire County Cricket Club to raise money they first played on the racecourse, by the cricket ground. It is strange to think that football clubs were seen as moneyspinners back in Victorian days, particularly to Derby supporters who had just been told that their club was over £30 million in debt. Problems at the racecourse arose when football fixtures had to be altered if they clashed with a horse race. To me this is staggering. I struggle to see the point of racing, and for many years have not considered it a sport since it seemed to exist purely for the benefit of bookies. However having had friends who have followed it and tried explaining its joys to me I am prepared to concede that it is almost a sport, but on a par with golf or synchronised swimming.

The new ground chosen was the sports ground built by Francis Ley for the workers at his castings factory. He had introduced baseball to his workforce after a trip to America, hence the name of the ground. Derby's first game here was in 1892, and they moved permanently in 1895.

It was quite nostalgic going into the ground, even though it was my first visit. It had the atmosphere of many grounds I had visited and was a proper football ground not a modern stadium. The four stands were all different and obviously had been built at different times, unlike modern stadiums that are all similar, with Middlesbrough, Derby and Stoke's grounds almost identical. Admittedly this does ignore the many huge advantages of modern stands. For

13

instance the only stand open to fans was the Toyota stand, formerly Co-op Stand, formerly Ley stand, formerly Popside Terrace. This was because it was the only one not made out of wood, highlighting a key reason for moving to new facilities.

It is rumoured that the site was originally a Gypsy site, and when they were forcibly evicted they cursed the club (who incidentally didn't even play there when the original sports ground was made). This will sound familiar to many football fans. Is there a club in a country that does not claim to be cursed (apart from Man Utd and Newcastle, whom some suspect have sold their souls to the devil)? Even Southampton's new St Mary's Stadium, opened in 2001, is supposedly cursed.

You have to wonder if in the manual of football ground building it says, "To choose a location first find a Gypsy encampment". It is no wonder that prejudice against Travellers is so high when millions of football fans wrongly blame them for years of frustration and disappointments.

However it is amusing to see what the evidence of the Baseball Ground curse is. In their first ten years there Derby County finished second and third in the league, reaching three FA Cup finals and four semi-finals. No wonder so many clubs were eager to get curses. To many this record would seem beyond their wildest dreams and would gain the team immortality, or freedom of the city/town at least, and a bit of underhand eviction would seem a small price to pay for such a 'curse'. Recently Bradford City had a civic reception and open top bus tour just for finishing 17th in the Premiership. So it seems that there have always been bad losers who cannot accept that they played badly and have to blame something else, like Alex Ferguson and 'the wrong colour shirts'.

I took my place ten minutes into the match, but I had to quickly move as it started raining on me, despite being eleven rows back. Perhaps old football grounds aren't as

14

good as I thought. The football was good though, with Derby the dominant side, building from the back with some neat passing. I saw a couple of Derby efforts well saved by Watford's goalkeeper but a goal was coming. A cross from the right was knocked towards the goal and the Derby number 4 (who I discovered was Lewis Hunt from peering over someone's shoulder to see their teamsheet) came and whacked it from just two yards out. The goalie, Lee, threw himself at it and managed to knock it up, but after what seemed an age and with everyone peering into the sky, it came down over the line. At this stage I presumed it was one-nil, after all the first few minutes are always quiet, aren't they? No, I was told it was two-nil. My paranoia for arriving late may be justified after all.

Perhaps they thought it was too easy, but Derby went to sleep on 39 minutes. Centre-back Youl Mawene didn't help his chances of a first team recall when he wandered away from Watford striker Godfrey. Suddenly Watford played a ball forward and it was a three-way race between Godfrey, Mawene and Derby's goalkeeper Andy Oakes, which Godfrey just won. He knocked it past Oakes and it trickled slowly into the net.

Half time gave me chance to take a good look at the ground without missing the action. It was looking a bit forlorn with 'The Rams' slogan on the opposite roof illegible unless you knew what to look for. Many of the advertising hoardings featured local businesses, unlike today's Premiership grounds that sell their boards collectively to national brands. Here were Jason Mason Paints, Leedale Plant Hire and Abbey Glass instead of Wash and Go and Ribena.

I could see fans wandering about, reminiscing about past glories, but I had none. Well, almost none. I had recently realised that a couple of favourite moments from the Match of the 70's series had come from Derby, although this hadn't registered at the time. The first was a punch up between Franny Lee and Billy Bremner when they had a real set to. This was no 'handbags at ten paces' as they both threw punch after punch. My Mum was surprised at me and my Dad laughing at such violence but we explained that one of the combatants was now a sober businessman and football club chairman.

The other amusing moment was the match in which they had to paint in the penalty spot. It appears that the Baseball Ground pitch had a reputation for being a quagmire, and on this occasion the spot had disappeared in all the mud. Everyone stood about wondering what to do until someone finally got a tape measure out. Joe Corrigan, Manchester City's goalkeeper, disputed the position but Derby duly scored it. The state of the pitch wasn't necessarily accidental, because Brian Clough used to regularly water the pitch at night. Before one European match he fell asleep whilst doing it and had to explain to an official why the pitch was waterlogged whilst there had been no rain outside a hotel three miles away!

The parochial nature of football clubs means that whilst we know all about our own club we only usually know fragments about other clubs. The players we consider to be massive legends are barely known by outsiders. For instance a book came into the library called Journey's With Jobey. Who was Jobey? Apparently he was manager for 20 odd years, but at least I hadn't embarrassed myself in front of Rams fans. Similarly, although I had heard of many 70's players I hadn't really heard of Charlie George. Yet here at Derby he is one of the all time greats to many fans.

The second half was not as good as the first. Perhaps the drizzle that had now set in was affecting the players. There were few chances, as moves seemed to break down well before they threatened the goals.

A 'celebratory' goal came a few minutes before time, when I witnessed one of the most blatant penalties I have ever seen. It was so blatant I couldn't believe what I saw.

16

A Watford defender simply pushed over striker Marvin Robinson in the box. Why he should do this I have no idea since there was no immediate danger, but the referee awarded the penalty. Robinson was all set to take it himself, but Hunt ran up and took the ball off him. I read the next day that Hunt had scored goal number one, so this was for his hat-trick. He took it well to make the score 3-1.

Derby 3 – 1 Watford
Hunt 6, 28, 85(pen) Godfrey 39

Derby: Oakes, Jackson, Grenet (Palmer 62), Hunt, Mawene (Molloy 72), Mills, Weckstrom, Boertien, Robinson, Tudgay, Twigg

Watford: Lee, Herd, J. Smith, Vernazza, Doyley, Ifil, Swonnell, Cook, Godfrey, Hughes (Blizzard 67), McNamee

Derby County v Preston North End
The Five Lamps, Duffield Road, Derby
Nationwide Football League Division One
Saturday 21 September 2002

Ten years on from the advent of mass football on Sky and we should have got used to strange kick-offs, but 5:45 on a Saturday tea time seemed to be the strangest still. This is the time of James Alexander Gordon and the Classified Results, checking the new league tables, poring over reports of other matches, and then 606. But he who pays the piper and all that...

I had come down to the Five Lamps on Duffield Road to watch the match. I felt an affinity with the name since my home town of Thornaby also has a Five Lamps area. It is strange how some names for area stick though, because the Five Lamps in Derby were only erected for a few years but 75 years later the name remained.

Times were desperate at Pride Park as they faced their biggest crisis since they nearly went bust in 1984. During the summer many fans were optimistic, and it continued into the season as they won their opening match. When I talked to Rams fan Mr Thompson, a regular customer at the library, he was quite confident that they could hold their own. This week though the club admitted that their debt was around £30 million and there seemed to be little chance of reducing it in the near future. Brian Richardson, former Coventry chairman, had been brought in to help raise money including selling players and getting a bond. So far neither had happened and he was running neck and neck with Nottingham Forest as to who was least popular in the city.

In the line up youngsters had almost replaced the foreign legion. Jim Smith had created a team of players

18

representing most corners of the globe. Costa Rican Paulo Wanchope, Italians Baiano and Eranio, Laursen from Denmark, German Schnoor, Croatian Igor Stimac, and Argentinean Carbonari being just a few examples. In their place were Bolder, Murray, and Boertien, all young and British but perhaps not as good.

Some, including Radio Derby summariser Ian Hall, blame the financial troubles on signing foreign players on long term contracts. They are seen as a cheaper option, but some don't work out, and you are then left with a few years left on a lucrative contract that you now cannot afford. Whilst it is a simplistic analysis, and where would we be without Johnny Foreigner to blame, Derby certainly were desperately trying to offload some of these players to save money.

Lack of economic realism was to blame, as Derby and many others failed to live within their means. ITV Digital was blamed for ruining clubs, but whilst what they did was despicable they only promised a maximum of a couple of million to clubs, which can't explain the £20+ million debts at Coventry, Bradford and others.

Partway through the first half a Preston defender went down under a heavy challenge. "What's the matter", a man in the pub shouted at the screen, "are you hurt, duck?" It is always a strange thing watching sport on TV. The temptation is to scream and shout at the players, despite the impossibility of them hearing anything. Back in 1990 Newcastle United started having a big screen at St James' Park to show some big away matches. Apparently the fans spent the first hour chanting and singing as usual before they began to realise that "Sing your hearts out for the lads" was over optimistic, and by the end they had all stopped. Four goals though from the Boro may have helped.

Jamaican international Ricardo Fuller shone out in the Preston side and kept testing the Derby defence. He had pace, skill and power, but also a frustrating tendency (for

Preston fans anyway) to get offside. The Derby County defence though stood firm for most of the first half, getting tackles in at the crucial moment. Unfortunately they couldn't quite manage to get through to half time. Fuller, always the most likely to break the deadlock beat Rams right-back Barton and ran along the goal line before knocking the ball back for Dickson Etuhu to score past Poom.

Seconds before the break Derby were dealt another blow, again from skipper Warren Barton. When Richard Cresswell was caught offside he caught the ball in an attempt to waste time and Barton took offence. Blood hurtled to his head as he wrestled Cresswell to the ground in his attempt to retrieve the ball, with the obvious consequences. It was one of those red cards that could easily be described as being for stupidity and left Derby with an even bigger mountain to climb.

The second half was not encouraging as Derby struggled to threaten to score. The mood in The Five Lamps was subdued. "A year ago we were shouting and screaming, now we can't be bothered", was the way one drinker summed up the mood. After all the struggles the fans seemed to expect the worst and few were expecting promotion this season even at this early stage. Crowds were very impressive with nearly 30,000 yet again but they seemed to be there out of duty. A Derby season ticket holder, Dorothy, had told me that going was like visiting the dentist.

Kinkladze had been marked out of the game. He had been in and out the team during his time at Pride Park and rarely got a run in the team. Many callers to Radio Derby called for him to be played more often, and their commentary team argued this too. As with many enigmas he could also be frustrating, but he still had more skill than any other Derby player. A common point people made was that whilst he didn't perform to his best every week, this was no worse than any other player. These sort of players split crowds, with some seeing the potential and prepared to overlook games where they don't perform, or else you see them as a luxury and prefer the players who are less skilful but seen to give 100%. The reasons why managers don't stick with him are known to Smith, Todd and Gregory, but when he is isolated without any support and service there is little he can do.

Not all the people in the pub were Derby supporters. As one or two people shouted encouragement after a bit of Derby pressure a voice cried out "Come on Preston".

The men on my right found this rather amusing for one simple reason. "Get the accent right", one of them called out as he realised that this was not a North End die-hard in our midst.

"Mad for it, come on Preston we're mad for it!" came the response. Anyone looking for a retort was spoiled for choice. "Why a Scouse accent?" another bloke called out. "Since when was Preston in Manchester?" a third man shouted.

Derby could only create a few half chances, and Lewis Hunt could not repeat his goalscoring feat that I had seen a few weeks earlier. The closest they came to an equaliser was a Riggott looping header that went just over from a corner. The match was virtually over on 76 minutes when after a Derby attack broke down Preston counter attacked McKenna on the edge of the Derby box passed the ball to his left for Healy to run onto and score easily. This time Mr Madforit's cheers were unanswered as he congratulated his newly adopted team.

The rest of the season didn't look promising. They were not good enough to get promotion straight back, with little threat to the opposition. However they shouldn't have to worry about relegation since they still looked fairly solid, and the back four certainly were not as weak as bottom defences sometimes are. A lot could depend on whether experienced and talented strikers Strupar and Ravanelli could come back and score goals. I had a feeling though that events of the field would take a back seat to financial problems.

Derby County 0 v 2 Preston North End
Etuhu 40, Healy 76

Derby: Poom, Barton (Captain), Boertien, O'Neil (Murray 81), Higginbotham, Riggott; Bolder (Hunt 45), Lee, Christie, Morris, Kinkladze Subs: Grant, Strupar, Evatt

Preston: Moilanen, Alexander, Lucketti, Edwards (Lewis 56), Murdock (Rankine 82), Broomes, McKenna, Skora, Etuhu, Cresswell, Fuller (Healy 70)

Attendance: Pub – 70, Pride Park – 29, 257

Long Eaton United v Shirebrook Town
Grange Park
Northern Counties East Division One
Saturday 28th September 2002

What do you know about Long Eaton? For most people the answer is very little, or nothing at all. For me, however, the only thing I knew about it until recently was that this was where Gary Birtles played before going on to Nottingham Forest, Manchester United and England. Why I should remember that from all those years I don't know. Perhaps it was because it was so unusual compared with the clubs other players were signed from. Alternatively it may just be because I specialise in knowing useless information. United don't seem as proud as I thought they might have done about Birtles, not even mentioning him in their potted history on their website.

Although Birtles was the reason I originally considered going to see Long Eaton, I was convinced that it was the game to see when I saw that Saturday brought a top of the table clash and local derby (incidentally the phrase comes from the horse race and not the city) with Derbyshire neighbours Shirebrook Town. Long Eaton were unbeaten in their six matches and top of the table, whilst Shirebrook were third having only been beaten once, by Mickleover Sports. Both teams had just been promoted from the Central Midland Alliance, level ten in the pyramid.

Long Eaton lies in the south east of Derbyshire, on the border with Nottinghamshire. In fact it is considered to be part of the Nottingham conurbation. A small agricultural town until the mid-nineteenth century, like many other places, it grew during the industrial revolution partly due to the lace industry and also due to its location. Transport links were excellent since it was on three rivers, Derwent,

Trent and Soar, and this was increased with opening of Derby canal and the convergence of various railway lines.

Shirebrook is not the most well known Derbyshire town. In The Derbyshire Guide it does not even get a mention. Until the discovery of coal a hundred years ago it was just another small agricultural village, but this discovery brought new people to the village, as well as a spiralling death rate from the usual Victorian diseases. From 1891 to 1901 the population shot up from 500 to 5,000. A book about the coal industry in Shirebrook, written in 1991, emphasises the importance of the colliery to village life and to the local economy. Local author Geoff Sadler wrote that he dreaded to think what would happen if the pit ever closed. A year later it did.

They do have some football pedigree even if the current club was relatively new. They have been home to many league footballers. Best of all they are one of only a handful of places in England to boast a World Cup winner, Ray Wilson having been born in Shirebrook.

United's Grange Park ground is in a quiet residential area. I walked down past the bowls club to the football ground and paid my £3 entrance fee. A committee member was pointing out to visitors some of the improvements that had been made. The clubhouse and dressing rooms were fairly new, and they had added floodlights and a fence. These may not seem much to those used to Premier League grounds, but I am learning that the little things at non-league grounds should never be underestimated. A mere fence enabled them to get promotion 17 years ago, and they were demoted from the NCE Premier League, one step up from where they are today, for not having floodlights. Even their current promotion was conditional upon enlarging the dugouts. Other clubs, such as Ilkeston have been known to change leagues due to ground regulations. The man was quite proud of what had happened, and the fact that with the children's teams there are now 200 players based at Grange Park.

I sometimes wondered how the different leagues varied in standard. Was there much difference between the pyramid levels, especially if Long Eaton and Shirebrook could both come up and top the league? I decided to ask the Gateman for his opinion. "Oh, it's a lot different", he told me, "it is a lot harder and faster for a start". I was going to ask him exactly how Long Eaton had got promoted when they had only finished third, but never got the chance as the Gateman optimistically said he had to deal with, "A last minute rush".

The game got off to a good start, with both teams creating chances. Long Eaton were playing in a nice navy blue strip with royal blue trim, unsurprising since they were nicknames the blues. Shirebrook played in red shirts with a black band across their chest.

The first goal came after nine minutes, when Shirebrook's Richard Flint hit a left wing free kick into the penalty area. Gareth Shipman stuck out a boot to strike it home. Unfortunately for him he was playing for Long Eaton. "Poor old Shippo", the fans near me muttered. It was the sort of moment that reporters used to say, "Would be on the next Danny Baker video". You know, the ones that feature footballing disasters and clangers. The first, presented by the named Mr Baker, was a success and like so many other ideas spawned many variations as Nick Hancock, Ron Atkinson and even Dickie Bird and Frankie Dettori got in on the act. I even saw one for darts! The market was soon saturated, and the quality went down as all the best clips were used up. Watching a fuzzy camcorder film of an obscure South American is not the same as laughing at Steve Bruce score an own goal for (or should that be against?) Man United.

Shirebrook were encouraged by the goal and dominated most of the half. Andy Carter went on the first of

25

his long runs deep into the Long Eaton half, but it was striker Steve Johnson who stood out. Not very big and fairly young, he could still handle himself and caused plenty of problems and won a number of free kicks and corners. When Long Eaton got the ball forward Shirebrook's Ian Streather and skipper Tony Starkey stood firm. In contrast Johnson and his colleagues were able to keep hold of it lot longer and usually until they could get a shot in. A minute after Johnson ran along the edge of the penalty area and forced a save, Long Eaton's Robbie Briscoe did the same, but his shot went wide. This seemed to sum up the first half.

At half time I got out my Walkman to get the Boro half time score. Unfortunately it was the Ryder Cup so football coverage went out the window. I may have already expressed my disregard for golf, but I do concede that people have a right to follow it (I am open minded and liberal like that) except when it gets in the way of me finding out the half time scores. Whoever was commentating was explaining how passionate a particular golfer was about golf. Not for the first time in my life I turned a radio off and pondered on the crazy world in which we lived.

The Blues were more fired up in the second half and created a number of openings, mostly via Briscoe who appeared to be their key player. Mark Hales in the Shirebrook goal had to push a couple of efforts out for corner, but the equaliser didn't come. Then Briscoe passed to Aaron Brady who went tumbling in the box, earning a yellow card for diving. "Fancy being booked for cheating", the Shirebrook manager called out innocently. Shirebrook even tried to help Long Eaton when Hales had to make a smart save to prevent a replay of the opening goal.

Shirebrook began to take control of the match again, with Flint as influential as ever. Not only did he take every set piece, delivering dangerous balls, he was also dominant in midfield and had a number of shots. He had a physical presence too, as one Blues player could testify to when he was elbowed by Flint. The referee took a lenient view and only awarded a free kick.

I was watching the match close to the dug outs and had the added bonus of getting a running commentary from the management teams. "That was a blatant foul, book him", one manager would scream. "That was dive, book him for cheating", the other would respond. Or words to that effect anyway. Do managers get trained in these blinkered ramblings? Does Arsene Wenger realise that nobody believes that he didn't see his player commit GBH on an opponent? I think it would be great if just for once the interviewer told him to stop lying.

Shirebrook scored again on 75 minutes. An opening was created for the dangerous Johnson, who hit it in from just inside the area. It was a just reward for an impressive performance, but his reward was substitution five minutes later.

Long Eaton had a final flourish and won a number of corners. Brady had a late effort when he cut in from the left and shot at the near post but Hales saved it. The action went to the other end when Flint won the ball and put Widdowson through. The goalie saved well but only push it out and a last ditch tackle was needed to avoid conceding another goal.

Late drama was still to come when Blues substitute Timson picked up his second yellow card and received his marching orders. Both bookings were for silly off the ball incidents but few fans were surprised. "He should have been sent off in a pre-season friendly", a nearby man told me, "but the Ref allowed him to be substituted instead". A minute later and it was full time and Shirebrook had deservedly won this top of the table clash to go top of the table.

Long Eaton Utd 0 v 2 Shirebrook Town
Shipman og. 9, Johnson 75

Long Eaton: Baker, Marston (Timson 46), Bray (McGinty), Gare, Dyce, Blasdale (Gordon 82), Heath, Shipman, Brady, Maxwell, Briscoe

Shirebrook: Hales, Wilson, Streather (Elgie), Wall, Starkey, Fisher, Flint, Shaw, Johnson (Widdowson 82), Orton, Carter

Borrowash Victoria v Hallam
The Robinson Construction Bowl
Northern Counties East Premier League
Saturday 12th October 2002

The names of stadiums can be quite evocative. When I was in Aberystwyth I went along a couple of times to Continental Park Avenue. I thought this was quite interesting, and conjured up images of foreign football tactics such as sweepers and an emphasis on slow build up, possession and passes rather than the full blooded English version. Or perhaps the ground had a Parisian street café in the ground. But no, the ground was so named because Continental Tyres sponsored the Seagulls. Oh well, another myth shot down.

Borrowash played at The Robinson Construction Bowl. This was in Spondon, but before people start forming campaigns and muttering about this being another Wimbledon and the dawn of 'franchise football' I had better point out that it is only a mile or so away from Borrowash at the Asterdale Sports and Leisure Club. This was also home to Derby City Rugby League FC, Spondon Bowls Club and various hockey and cricket clubs. The Bowl was described as "very impressive" in the programme. Not the words that immediately sprang to mind, but not too bad all things considered even if the idea of hospitality on the hut that bore that name was not very tempting. The encircling earth banks though did make it feel a little like a bowl.

I asked the two men on the gate how the Vics were doing at the moment. "Not very well", I was told, "but you can't expect much from a team of youngsters and new signings. He explained that most of last year's team had gone to Heanor Town, a team two levels below Borrowash. The reason was money, with players there rumoured to be on £70 or so a man. I may be naïve but I was surprised that an entire team would choose to drop that far. "All today's players want to know what money they are being offered", one of them told me, "When I played I just wanted to play football, preferably with my friends. I got £2 a match when I played for Newhall but that didn't matter." Never having been in the position of having to choose between those options I was unqualified to judge.

I wandered over to the front of the grandstand, where most of the spectators (a dozen or so) were stood. Paying the players anything was amazing considering that there must have been less than a hundred paying £3.50 or less. Not for the first time I was impressed at how much a club like this could achieve, and was a little embarrassed by my first reaction to the ground.

It was obvious from early on that this match was going to be effort over style. Borrowash were playing in red and white striped shirts and black shorts, whilst Hallam wore blue and white hooped shirts, so imagine Sheffield United versus QPR. Borrowash played five at the back (or three depending on how you describe the system). Neither side succeeded in stringing more than couple of passes together and it was easy to understand the Gateman's low expectations for the season and the low ambition of just staying up. After ten minutes the locals started cheering as five passes were played between Borrowash players. Wingbacks Alderson and Banks looked the most comfortable on the ball.

Hallam then created a couple of chances, a cross going right across the edge of the six yard box without anyone getting a touch, and a few minutes later another cross was caught by Vics goalie Steve Smith, before Hallam striker John Tesh shoulder charged him over the goal line. Tesh did his best to look surprised when the referee gave a free kick instead of a goal. "Nat Lofthouse", the crowd shouted as one. What Nat thinks of being known primarily for that dodgy goal instead of one of England's greatest footballers I can only wonder. The one time record England goalscorer and member of one of England's greatest attacks is best known today for barging a goalkeeper into the net.

A chap came over with his radio. "How's Derby doing?" everyone asked. "Nil Nil", he replied. "At least they aren't losing", one man commented, showing how much confidence Rams fans currently had. "Scotland are winning", radioman told us. "I don't believe it, are they playing the Scilly Isles?" It is hard to fathom Scotland's drop in form that made us so sceptical of their lead over Iceland. Fifteen years ago they had Dalglish, Durie, Speedie, McAvennie, Nicholas, Johnston and Nevin, yet today they struggle to name a half-decent forward.

Chances came sporadically to both sides; Alderson heading clear under pressure, before forcing the Hallam goalie to fumble his free kick minutes later. Borrowash even managed a spell of pressure, the highlight being a shot that hit the post.

You may wonder what right I have to be critical, and you'd have a point. I never even got into my primary school team. In fourth year juniors I stayed behind for the trials, along with 25 other hopefuls. To finish with there was a practice match. I was the only one not to get a go in that match. Now I could sue Thornaby C of E School for emotional cruelty, or just say that Miss Jackson hated me and overlooked a potential football genius, as my dreams were destroyed at the tender age of ten. To be fair I was rubbish and had no skill, although the bit about Miss Jackson hating me was true.

Still, some fans have rather more right to be critical. Many years ago at Ilkeston they were a man short so asked a spectator to play. Of course he had to score didn't he. I am sure that he was unbearable on the terraces after that, regaling everyone with that match.

At half time I read up the notes on Hallam. They are the second oldest football club in the world, after neighbours

Sheffield FC, which is a pretty impressive boast. They looked to be a well-supported club judging by the number of fans they had brought. Well, this is all in relative terms but they probably had as many supporters here as Borrowash did. Their other claim to fame was that Howard Wilkinson used to play for them. However there was discontent on the terraces (OK, two people mumbling) over the inaccuracy of the notes. They were four days out of date because he was now Sunderland manager instead of FA Technical Director.

Ten minutes into the second half came the opening goal, via the penalty spot. Vics forward Tom Widdison was fouled and Steve Banks hit the spot kick into the top right hand corner of the net. The home side may have taken the lead, but there was barely a clap, let alone cheer.

This spurred Hallam into action. They seemed slightly more likely to score all afternoon, and this was the incentive they needed to turn this into goals. Steve Capill went on a surging run into the penalty area and blasted it past Smith to equalise within a minute.

The game was now transformed far beyond the poor first half and within a minute Hallam nearly conceded an own goal, and another minute later Banks gave Bestwick a good opportunity but he shot wide.

Hallam were not impressed by some refereeing decisions. They may have been sponsored by Camus, but centre back Maybury (former Alfreton player manager apparently) was not very philosophical. It was no surprise when the referee finally booked him for dissent.

Both sides had good chances, but the biggest drama was saved for the 80th minute. Steve Smith in the Borrowash goal caught the ball from a corner, and was promptly fouled by a Hallam player. Smith then turned and kicked the aggressor. He didn't have the excuse of "I was going for the ball", "I mistimed my tackle", or any other excuse. The red card was inevitable. We now had a discussion on the touchline as to the rules. Had play stopped? Was it a penalty? Which foul would take precedence? No one was very sure. Fans like to tell everyone how well they understand the game, the rules, tactics and intricacies. When a referee makes a decision we can all disagree and let him know what he should have done. However whilst waiting for a decision no one sounded confident, which was embarrassing.

Play was restarted with a free kick to Borrowash, giving them a chance to hold on. Hutchings, who had put on the goalkeeper's jersey and gloves, had his first save to make two minutes later, when he blocked a corner. Borrowash booted the ball clear every opportunity, but with no release valve it inevitably came straight back. Eventually the referee blew for full time and they had hung on for a draw.

Borrowash Victoria 1 v 1 Hallam
Banks 55   Capill 56

Borrowash: Smith, Alderson (Walton 34), Banks, Carlin, Rigley, Strzyewski, Freeman, Hutchings, Widdison, Bestwick, Johnson

Hallam: Spooner, Hayes, Wells, Maybury, A.N. Other (Naylor 26), Clarke, Tesh, Tibbenham, Gates, Capill, Hill

Mickleover Sports v Worsbrough Bridge
Station Road
Northern Counties East Division 1
Saturday 2nd November 2002

I had a quick panic during the week. I was on the verge of getting a ticket for the Chesterfield v Barnsley match when I realised it was a 12:15 kick off, and I finished work at one o'clock. After a quick check of the fixture lists I decided on a trip to Station Road. Mickleover is now one of many suburbs that are part of the City of Derby. Not so long ago it was just a village and there are plenty of photographs of the main road through looking like a rural track.

Until 1982 they were called Mickleover Old Boys and played in the local leagues. A bit of ambition later and a move to Station Road and they joined the Central Midland League. A gradual but continual improvement saw them overtake Mickleover Royal British Legion as the top Mickleover team and as champions in 1999 they were promoted to the Northern Counties East League division one. Top five finishes in the last three seasons brought optimism of further promotions.

Station Road is on the very edge of Mickleover and the Derby City boundary. The clubhouse/dressing rooms reminded me of Long Eaton's, and had been opened in 1992. Surrounded by fields on two sides, giving it a rustic feel, I could see a barn in the distance. The barn, however, did not have a door, perhaps deliberately to prevent a series of jokes about out of form forwards being unable to hit the said agricultural storehouse opening device.

The other thing that I noticed was the tannoy. Quiet and sparingly used at the last two grounds I had visited, I was met here with the booming strains of "When no-one else can understand me, when everything I do is wrong…"

No, it wasn't Adam Crozier doing karaoke, but a 'Best of the 1960's' CD. I wasn't sure what to make of the FA Chief Executive's departure. Some of the modernisation was good, helping to replace the stuffy image of the FA. The increase in prize money to non-league clubs in the FA Cup was another notable achievement. However like most football fans I was cautious about the shambolic Wembley revamp and reform such as a foreign England manager. However it has to be said that anyone who counts Ken Bates as an enemy has to have something going for him.

The rain continued to fall and we all huddled in the main stand apart from one hardy spectator who stood at one end beneath his umbrella. Some ladies on the back row had even brought rugs. Mickleover, playing in red and white shirts and black shorts that were almost identical to nearest neighbours Borrowash Victoria, were still getting settled when Worsbrough scored. A defence splitting ball from the left found Alvey ten yards out and he hit the ball into the bottom left hand corner.

Mickleover hit back a few minutes later when Karl Payne passed to Carl Cunningham. Worsbrough defenders stopped and appealed for offside, and perhaps Cunningham was distracted by this because he paused for what seemed like an age. Perhaps I'm being unfair and he was simply composing himself, fully aware of the situation, but whatever the truth was he ended his staring contest with the goalkeeper and scored.

Ten minutes gone and already two goals, I was looking forward to the rest of the match. After the Borrowash match I was not sure what standard of football to expect, especially with the weather. The chap sitting behind me, Charlie, said that Mickleover usually played good football, and I was quite impressed by what I was seeing. Both sides played decent football and created chances. Sports' Wood had a good header saved, but the action tore down to the other end and ex-Derby County trainee Mark Wilson showed lightning reactions to save a shot that flew at him from the edge of the penalty area (Yes, I know that any shot that is off the ground could be said to fly, but I am using the word/cliché to imply the above average power used to propel the ball).

I was even more impressed by the football that followed. Ross Mays tried an audacious back heel to a colleague as he went down the left wing. I was not surprised when Bridge (apologies to Worsbrough if that is not your nickname) intercepted this fancy bit of play, but Mays immediately went and won it back. The ball was passed over to the right wing and the excitement in the stand was rising as the attack neared the box. The final ball was played into the area and Karl Yeoman hit it...over. Unfortunately he had to stretch a bit too far and he couldn't quite control his shot. A 'goal of the month' was missed.

Of course it couldn't last and as the rain drizzled down the match became bittier. Sports did have a few more chances before half time; the best being a header from Cunningham which Bridge goalie Bowman (who was also Assistant Manager) fumbled the ball on the line. "Goal", we all (except Worsbrough people obviously) cried from our perfect vantage point 80 odd yards away, but it hadn't crossed the line. The officials denied Sports a penalty too when the referee decided that a rather obvious push on Cunningham was too obvious. After declaring the Derby penalty in August as the most blatant I had seen, I had seen some other close contenders as teams seemingly tried to win this award.

As half time approached the drizzle turned into incessant rain. What a dilemma – do I stay in my seat in the dry, or go into the rain to get a tea to warm me up? I opted for the latter, but not before hearing the tannoy announcer ask someone with a Walkman to write down the scores for him. My image of these people surrounded with the world of football news and the very latest scores at their fingertips was shattered.

The second half saw Mickleover continue to dominate but Bridge still threatened on the counter attack. Sports had most possession but found it hard to make it count. Even when they got the ball into the box they struggled to get a shot in.

It was still throwing it down and players had to gradually slow down before turning or moving in different directions. "Don't make such heavy weather of it", Charlie called out. We laughed. The boundary of the pitch though began to resemble mini canals and the linesman in front of us had to run a couple of feet either side of the line to avoid wading.

The raffle seller made his appearance and he was obviously the right man for the job. "Don't be so mean", he said to one person who refused. "If you can afford a burger you can afford a ticket", he said to another. When one man said he didn't drink (the prize was a bottle of something alcoholic) Mr Raffleman said he was tea total himself and that was no excuse. He could have probably got Saddam Hussein to contribute to a whip round for George W. Bush. It was entertainment in a section of play that was quiet with both teams struggling in the incessant rain.

On the pitch there was a moment of high farce when after a free kick to Mickleover the players faced each other from a gap of inches for 30 seconds before the referee came in to push each side back a few yards. When it was eventually taken Wayne Sutton, or Sooty as we in the know call him affectionately, had a good shot pushed over. The squabble continued however and when Cunningham was fouled a lady a few seats along stood up and screamed, "Get your hands off him", looking like those old wrestling matches when old ladies went in the ring to hit the baddies with handbags. The wrestling analogy continued when Yeoman and Bridge's Boreham ignored the ball and grappled with each other on the floor. Amazingly they were only booked.

"Can you all hear", a voice boomed out. It was Mr Raffleman back with the draw results. When a cheer came from one man Mr Raffleman was not impressed; "If you have won it I'll bloody kill you". I suppose intimidating people into not accepting their prize would be one way of increasing the profits!

Bev Hudson, no relation, a Sports player for over nine years, hit a shot wide when he slipped at the crucial moment. Fellow sub Leighton blazed over, Stevens carefully lifted the ball over a melee of players but over the bar too, and centre back Reynolds came forward to head a ball directly at the goalie. The kitchen sink had been thrown at the Bridge goal but it was still all-square. Worsbrough had a late flourish and could almost have had a winner against the run of play but failed to score too.

The referee blew for full time and we all dashed the short distance to the clubhouse for the final scores on TV. The Sports physio summed the mood up when he said, "We should have won it."

Mickleover Sports 1 v 1 Worsborough Bridge

Cunningham 10   Alvey 4

Mickleover: Wilson, Yeoman, Salloway (Hudson 70), Wood, Reynolds, Sutton, Stevens, Ault (Warren 80), Cunningham, Payne, Mays (Leighton 50)

Worsborough: Bowman, Prica, West, Alvey (Burrell 75), Handley, Renshaw, Taylor, Boreham, Wilkinson, Jackson, Turner. Subs Mitchell, Lees

Bonfire Night saw both teams back at Station Road for the Presidents Cup. This time Mickleover managed to take their chances and won 5-1. Not for the first time I was left wishing I had chosen my matches differently! Both teams changed their sides, and teenager Dave Middleditch came in to score a hat trick, with Payne grabbing the other two goals.

Heanor Town v Studley
The Town Ground
FA Vase
Saturday 9th November 2002

Although it was not the most beautiful morning ever seen, it was dry, so the Cup game was still on. Heanor is a town 10 miles north east of Derby on the Nottingham border, near The American Adventure theme park (where no doubt it is obligatory to carry at least one gun at all times). Unlike some of the places I was visiting this season, I was quite familiar with Heanor, having gone there regularly for work meetings over the past few months. My first visit however was at midnight on a foggy night the previous February, when I was part of a crack burglar alarm disabling squad. But that is another story...

Although it was and had been home to many industries, coal mining had played a major part in its past and for a time Heanor were nicknamed the Miners. A town guide (written in the optimistic 1960's when a new dawn of world peace, eternal prosperity and modernism seemed just around the corner if you believed the writers) claimed Mary Howitt as the most famous resident, so famous, it said, that we don't need to say any more about her. Have you heard of her? No, neither had I. It is quite embarrassing when you have never heard of a local hero. If you admit your ignorance in front of natives they take offence, just like I do if people do not know about James Cook. I did investigate and discovered that Mary wrote the poem "Come into the parlour, said the spider to the fly".

The football club had existed on and off since 1883. Although most clubs had financial trouble Heanor appeared to have more than most. In 1907 they went bankrupt despite attendances of over 2,000. Twenty years later they only survived to the end of the season by one of the most ingenious and audacious solutions imaginable, getting other teams to give them money and pay their travelling costs! Perhaps Derby County directors could take note and see if other Division One clubs would give them a few pounds or pay their coach costs and hotel bills. However Portsmouth had beaten them to it and got Premiership clubs to loan them players whilst paying most of the wages. An attempt to do the same with Derby's Ravenelli only failed when the Football League blocked it.

I got to the Town Ground in good time and chatted to the programme seller about the club's situation. "We're doing quite well this season", he said, "and playing some good football. Just a shame about our facilities". The ground was shared with the cricket club, with the wicket adjacent to the football pitch. The clubhouse and changing rooms had seen better days and the only covered area was just a very basic shelter for perhaps 50 people. By the entrance stood a boarded up brick building. "The Council are supposed to be building us new facilities with a new stand and dressing rooms. They have been saying that for years though". Over the borough border at Ilkeston there had been similar problems battling to get the relevant local authority landlords to provide the necessary support.

Two large piles of sand were pointed out to me, which I was told had recently been delivered by Amber Valley Borough Council in readiness for work this month. The sand was causing quite a stir. "It's Heanor beach!" one man said as he came through the turnstile. "I'll go back to get my bucket and spade and we can build sandcastles", another chap said. A third man, holding a black and white umbrella remarked that there was more interest in this sand than there was in the match. Being so far from the seaside may have had something to do with this attitude, as well as scepticism of the Council, who owned the ground. They had apparently demolished the only stand five years ago saying it was unsafe, built the covered area as a temporary one year measure, and done nothing since. Mr

Umbrellaman's umbrella was necessary for anyone wanting to stand on the popular side during the rain.

Still, the reason I had come was not two piles of sand but the match, round two of the FA Vase. To follow non-league football you had to understand the complexities of cup competitions. Everyone enters the FA Cup, well, most clubs anyway. The other competitions were just for certain teams. League Cups were fairly obvious, as were County Cups. The FA Trophy was for Conference Clubs and the next two rungs of the Pyramid below. The FA Vase seemed to be for the clubs below that, up to North Counties East League and other leagues at that level. Then came floodlit cups, the previously mentioned President's Cups, and the Wilkinson Sword Trophy. There must be some interesting duels in that last competition! Even looking at a full list of entrants sometimes left you scratching your head as to why clubs in one division took part and others didn't.

Cups were an important part of football life and could bring a bit of glamour to a season. Even if you are struggling in the league or you can't get promoted due to red tape you could always beat the bigger clubs. In your dreams anyway. Football fans are big dreamers and endure years of affliction for one big result. In Anton Rippon's book on Derbyshire Football each club's record in the FA Cup is given greater prominence than their league records.

The Lions, named after the town's 1920's carnival band, had a good record reaching the last 32 three times, although these were all in the 1890's. More recently they had reached the first round proper twice, if the 1950's and 1960's can be called recent that is. In terms of actually winning trophies the Derbyshire Senior Cup was the most profitable, winning it four times in a row in the 1960's. Their record in the Vase wasn't too bad. Mr Programme-man was looking forward to today's clash, "We've got a good reputation. I've seen us knock a few bigger clubs out over the years."

Whether this had affected the attendance, or not, I can't say but compared with the last three matches I had gone to there was a decent crowd and atmosphere. The £3 entrance fee was too much for one fan though who climbed in over a wall. I should point out that it was not a youngster but a middle-aged man.

Studley were undaunted by the giant killing reputation and dominated from the first minute. Strikers Crisp and Coppin had a hatful of chances each, but contrived to put the ball wide or else Dean Lowe pulled off a great save. Even Diego Forlan would have been embarrassed not to have scored; well perhaps they weren't that bad. The worst was Coppin's header wide when he was virtually under the crossbar.

"We must be playing for penalties", one Heanor fan concluded. The trouble was that Heanor couldn't seem to hang on to possession. When they managed to get the ball away they would pass it straight to an opponent hit it into touch or be dispossessed. Studley were two levels up in the pyramid, in the Midland Alliance, and the difference in class showed. Heanor may have been affected by an injury a fortnight ago to Wes Armstrong, their star player, because there was little creativity. The Lions however did not live up to their nickname and did not seem 'up for it'. Attack and attack came but they could do little to stop it.

Heanor managed four efforts in the first half, the best being a free kick by centre-back Pete Davis that looked as if it had gone in, but had hit the side netting instead. The natives were getting restless though as simple passes went astray and Studley continued to create chances. Mr Programme-man had told me that Lowe was possibly the best player in the team, and he lived up to this reputation with a phenomenal save. Coppin couldn't believe it when he headed down from a couple of years out only for the goalkeeper to dive down and push the ball away. Who knows, we all knew enough about football to know that a fluky goal from Heanor and anything could happen, couldn't it?

Half time brought reprieve for Heanor. Against the odds they were still level. As usual I was struggling to get the results I wanted from the radio. Although I hadn't heard of Mary Howitt, I had heard of two former Heanor players, Nigel Pearson and Lindy Delapenha, who may both have also played for a particular club. Pearson had slipped through the nets of youth scouts and played for the Lions before Shrewsbury Town bought him. He went on to have a great career, with Ron Atkinson calling him the best captain he had known.

Delapenha's spell at the Town Ground was at the end of his career. Jamaican born Delapenha came to Britain to do national service and became the first overseas black footballer to play league football. He achieved legendary status during his 9 seasons at Ayresome Park after one of those matches that people who were there tell everyone for the rest of their lives. In a derby match with Sunderland Delapenha took a penalty. He had one of the hardest shots in football and the ball carried on into the back of the net and under it. Despite showing the referee that the net was not fastened down properly the goal was still not given.

A Pearson or Delapenha was desperately required by today's team as Studley continued where they had left off. Eventually Lowe and a defender had a mix up and the number 11 tapped the ball in. The goal scorer proceeded to strip off and tear round the pitch for the next few minutes in a way that would make snooker's Peter Ebdon look restrained. If there is random drug testing in the FA Vase he could be in trouble. What he would have done if he had scored a spectacular goal I dread to think.

A bit more urgency crept into Heanor's play as they introduced substitutes and they began to create a few chances. Captain Matt Johnson looked to have equalised

44

with a strong header but it went straight to the Studley goalie. Long serving Paul Mable, on as substitute, had opportunities ranging from a looping header that almost went in to a shot from the edge of the box and went out of the ground.

I should point out that at the games I write down incidents in a notebook before typing them up later. Occasionally I struggle to interpret what I wrote. A note for the 88th minute appears to say *'cat shot at goalie'!* The last few minutes were eventful but not that eventful. Only a minute after whatever happened Studley wrapped it up. A Studley sub dribbled into the box but was forced wide. When he lost the ball Mark Crisp made up for his misses with a goal from the tightest of angles.

"You're rubbish like the Albion, rubbish like the Albion", cried out a few Lions fans. The Studley management team looked quite pleased and said that they quite admired West Brom. "No, Burton Albion you idiot", one of the fans screamed. The referee brought proceedings to a close before an in depth discussion over the relative league positions of the relevant clubs could ensue. Dreams of Wembley (or wherever hosts the final now) were over for another year for Heanor. They could once again concentrate on the league.

Heanor 0 v 2 Studley
Neath 55
Crisp 89

Heanor: Lowe, Thomas, Travis (Fowler 68), Johnson, Preston, Davis, Froggatt, Townsend, Sharp, Flanagan (Henson 62), Shipley (Mable 62)

Studley: Pugh, Keight, Davis, Beddowes, Hands, Mitchell, Grubb (Johnson 74), Kavanagh, Crisp, Coppin (Turk 90), Neath (Cross 78)

Att: 70

Chesterfield v Huddersfield Town
Saltergate
Nationwide Football League Division 2
Saturday 30th November 2002

An Englishman was introducing the American lady sitting on the other side of the train to the local delights, although whether they knew each other beforehand I don't know. "This is the Peak District", he proudly told her. "How lovely", she gasped, looking at the landscape covered by a thin layer of autumn mist. I'm not sure if this particular area near Ambergate was the Peak District, it certainly wasn't inside the National Park, and the bit we were going through was not exactly Dovedale or Snake's Pass, but I could empathise. I like the countryside, and although most people prefer summer I personally think a bit of autumnal colour and atmosphere just sets it off nicely.

As we approached Chesterfield Mrs Americanwoman was being told of the town's best-known feature the crooked spire of St Mary's church. She was enthralled as she was told about the legend of how the spire got its crook. However I like debunking myths so I won't tell you that the devil landed on the spire one day, sneezed from the incense and caught the spire with his tail as he fell off. Nor will I say that the spire turned to see a virtuous bride getting wed and it will straighten out if another virtuous bridge ever weds at St Mary's. Instead I will tell you that it is twisted and warped, not crooked, probably due to the unseasoned wood they used, and there are six such spires in Great Britain and 52 in Europe.

Like any good local landmark/hero most local businesses try to incorporate the word spire into their title. We have Spire Vets, Spire Hair Dressers, Spire Hydraulics, and Spire Cafe. In total 23 companies call themselves

Spire something or other. The club is also nicknamed the Spirites.

I headed into town to find The Barley Mow hostelry to meet some people I had never met or seen before. I had posted a message on a Spirite internet message board for inside information on how the team was doing and who the players to watch out for were. I had a couple of responses from some very friendly people (even after I told them I supported Boro) and was kindly invited to join in a get together for regular posters (people who post messages on the board as opposed to a meeting for normal sized pieces of paper that advertise events). I went into the crowded pub and wondered what to do. There was nothing for it but to go round everyone I could see and ask them if they had heard of the names I had been given. I think I know how a spy feels as they use code words in a Cold War movie. "Fruitflies are indigo", or some such subtle password. Most people shook their heads and gave me a strange look as they tried to work out how many pints I must have had.

I discovered that evening that my contact had decided not to come after some threatening postings by other chatters. The internet has become a valuable part of life for supporters. Message boards allow supporters from anywhere in the country to communicate, sometimes anonymously, with people they would never normally meet. Many have led to friendships and even marriage. It seemed a shame that despite the parties all being big Chesterfield supporters some people had taken things a bit too far. Mark had come across to me as a good bloke but had obviously taken the criticism to heart.

After a while I headed for Saltergate. It gets its name from one of the important commodities that was transported through the town from Cheshire since Roman times. Chesterfield is Derbyshire's second largest town and grew partly from the trade routes and markets. A charter in 1204 gave it the exclusive right to hold a market in the area, long before the European Union investigated monopolies and cartels. Lead, tanned products, animals and agricultural products were some of the items sold there. A canal and three early railways all ensured Chesterfield's prominence continued well into the Nineteenth century.

As the county's second town it is appropriate that it also boats the county's second highest team. For most of their existence (debate rumbles on as to whether it dates from 1866 or 1919) they have yo-yoed between divisions three and four (or equivalents) with just a few years in division two. One claim to fame, and one which had been highlighted weekly at the start of the season was their run of scoring in 46 consecutive matches in 1926/27, a record almost overtaken this year by Arsenal. The biggest trophy won was the Anglo-Scottish Cup in 1981. No sniggering at the back, I'll have you know that it is a very prestigious cup to many clubs. On their way they beat the mighty Rangers before defeating Notts County in the final.

More recently they claimed national headlines by getting to the FA Cup semi-finals. For a second (old third) division club this was dreamland, as they knocked out first division Bolton and Premiership Nottingham Forest. The semi-final at Old Trafford, in front of 60,000 fans goes down as a classic. Many have said it was greatest game they have seen, as the plucky underdogs went two nil up against ten-man Middlesbrough. A controversial Chesterfield 'goal' (for any Chesterfield fans reading it didn't matter that the ball crossed the line – it was disallowed for an infringement. Sorry to have to emphasis that) before Boro drew level and took the lead in extra time. Seconds from the end a Jamie Hewitt header looped in to force a replay that seemed unthinkable two hours earlier. Boro cruised to a 3-0 win the next week but Chesterfield had had the greatest moment in their history, won the nation's hearts and sympathy and Boro were once again portrayed as the villains!

By the time I got to the ground the misty autumnal day had turned into a wet day. After the last few matches I'd attended it was a good feeling to be in a crowd. The Kop, in which I was standing, was fairly full, as was most of the ground. On my left was a singly storey stand, and on the right was the main stand, a raised wooden single storey stand. Opposite was an uncovered terrace, which, you guessed it, in the traditions of football the visitors were left in the elements. I suppose it was not too surprising considering the home fans fund most of the ground improvements. I thought the ground looked OK, but two Yorkshiremen I met later both named Saltergate as the worst ground they had visited, although they may have changed their minds if they ever dried out!

Match sponsor was Chatsworth House, rather a cut above Smith's Fish and Chips or most sponsors. I'd read that the Duke of Devonshire was Club President, but wasn't sure how active he was and had perhaps wrongly assumed it was just an honorary title. Perhaps his Grace was in the Kop leading the chanting!

Chesterfield, down to their last 14 professionals, dominated the opening exchanges and kept the ball in the Huddersfield half for the first five minutes. Former Huddersfield player Rob Edwards had the first chance, a long-range shot that only just missed. For all their dominance they struggled to create clear openings. The visitors occasionally threatened, mainly when the Chesterfield defence didn't mark tight enough.

On the half-hour mark Payne made a crucial tackle on the edge of the Spirite penalty area. He broke and released Hurst who sprinted up the field and fired a shot from 30 yards out that was pushed round for a corner. Sustained pressure paid off three minutes later when from a left wing corner Kevin Dawson stabbed the ball in from eight yards out when centre-back Mathias failed to control the ball.

The conditions were tricky and left back Howson appeared to have dropped a clanger as he slipped in his own area to let Worthington in but Howson managed to get up and make a great tackle before he could shoot. Huddersfield kept the ball at that end for a few minutes and Blatherwick, who I had been told was a key player at the back, made an outstanding tackle. Chesterfield hung on relatively comfortably for half time.

Half time brought my usual attempt to find the half time scores. Radio 5 was not blathering on about golf or rugby union for a change, but I couldn't get good reception on my radio and I had to overcome a loud tannoy system. Eventually the Chesterfield announcer read out the scores "Brought to you by Bloggs Estate Agents". What did he mean? Perhaps it was similar to at Mickleover, except in this instance the estate agent staff sat in their office noting down scores and telephoning them through. Or perhaps not.

For the second half Huddersfield had made a change. Mick Wadsworth was rumoured to be heading for the sack if they didn't win and he had to do something. Is the name familiar? For those of you who have not read the chapters in order I have already mentioned that he played for Alfreton. He also played for Buxton and was player-manager of Matlock for two games before being called upon to coach England's youth and under 21 teams. No disrespect to Ernie Moss but it is hard to imagine the Sven Goran Eriksson and the FA heading to Matlock Town for a replacement when David Platt leaves.

Wadsworth opposite number, Dave Rushbury, must be one of the few club physios to have been appointed manager. His former job is now held by another ex-Chesterfield player, Jamie Hewitt, so perhaps it might happen again. It was he who grabbed the headlines five years ago by heading the last gasp equaliser at Old Trafford.

The change, which involved going from three centre backs to a 4-4-2 formation, may have worked because it was Huddersfield who had the early chances. Carl Muggleton saved well from a long-range shot. "England's number one, England England's number one", sang out the fans. A bit optimistic, but Chesterfield does have a reputation of producing top class goalkeepers. Gordon Banks, Steve Ogrizovic and Scotland's Jim Brown all played at Saltergate, and John Lukic and Bob Wilson were both born in the town. Muggleton, in his third spell at the club could boast an England u21 cap on his CV. Play soon resembled the first half though with Chesterfield looking the stronger side.

The fans who had e-mailed me all said that Hurst and Brandon were the men to watch, and it was easy to see why. Both were pacy and everytime a ball was played through they seemed to cruise past defenders. They also had a fair amount of skill, Brandon showing this early in the second half with a lovely run from the right wing into the box. The change in formation by Huddersfield had allowed them both more room to display their skills, but despite their ability the score remained the same. Both players could create chances but they were unable to put them away. Twice in a few minutes Chris Brandon took the ball into the box before shooting wide, and then shortly after he beat the full back to send in a cross that was nowhere near a blue shirt. Although I would not perhaps agree with Mark that they were worth the entrance fee alone, they were certainly good to watch.

One of the best chances for Chesterfield to increase their lead came on 58 minutes when Brandon went on a great run. Running into the box he looked odds on to score but seemed to be in two minds and after a slight pause he hit it wide. Headers from the centre backs Blatherwick and the impressive Steve Payne were good and would have been goals if they had not been straight at the shaven headed Bevan.

51

As the game went quiet the drama was reserved for the terraces. Someone had obviously thought that it would be fun to bring in a foghorn. For most of the time it was just an occasional blast to accompany a chant, but then the owner got more confident and decided on a five-minute fog horn solo. A few shouts didn't deter them, and he/she was not even embarrassed by a few hundred fellow fans chanting at him/her to shut up. Then there was silence, followed seconds later by a clatter at the back. We all turned to see the offending item lying on the ground before we let out the second biggest cheer of the day.

We hadn't missed much on the pitch. Chesterfield tried hard but still couldn't score again. Hurst went on another good run but hit a tame shot at the keeper when others were in a better position. Soon after he went down under an innocuous challenge in the area and earned a booking for diving.

As happens at so many football matches, one side dominates, but then has to hang on tight for the last five minutes. Huddersfield suddenly tried hard for the unlikely and undeserved equaliser. Terrier's midfielder Kenny Irons hit the post before substitute Thorrington hit a good chance wide. Chesterfield were not to be denied though and the points were safe.

On the train back I read The Times' Sports section. Leeds financial trouble was one of the main stories. I had been trying to link in a subject to just one match to avoid endlessly repeating comments about referees, state of grounds or whatever else I ramble on about. The same went for financial trouble. Every club goes through it at some stage, and usually on a frequent cycle. Alfreton, Ilkeston and Derby spring to mind immediately. Chesterfield though seem to have caused their bank manager more sleepless nights than most.

The latest trouble came just a year after their profitable FA Cup semi-final appearance. They had been in trouble in the late 1987 too, and had only just recovered from debts run up by manager Arthur Cox in the early 1980's (Derby fans may sympathise at this point). It isn't just in recent times, because in a programme from 1963 fans are told that the club is in trouble and needed help, even in putting up players. There's a thought, imagine putting out a call to fans today to see if anyone has a spare room Ravanelli could sleep in!

The solution has often been to call on the fans. The old Supporters Club had a clause that said they could transfer surplus funds to the club, and in the Chesterfield Town's first season in the league there was a loss so they had a bazaar! Many ground improvements only took place from funds raised by the supporters club, so it is appropriate that the new owners of the club are the fans.

I have seen much frustration at clubs being owned by egomaniacs who couldn't care less about a team. Before any chairman sues me I should point out that they are an exception, and I am talking about how they are perceived. For the last 13 years I have been a member of the Football Supporters Association who campaign for a bigger say by fans in the running of the game. Fans actually running the club is an unexpected bonus and surely this is the ideal solution? Well, perhaps not. Looking at the internet message boards they are just as full with rumour, counter-rumour and disgruntled supporters. I am casting no judgement on the CSFT since I know very little. Perhaps it is just in the nature of football fans that they will always blame the referee, pass on the latest rumour within seconds of hearing it (or making it up), know more than the manager about tactics and moan at whoever is in charge of the club.

Chesterfield 1 v 0 Huddersfield Town
Dawson 33

Chesterfield: Muggleton; Dawson, Blatherwick, Payne, Howson; Booty, Ebdon, Edwards; Brandon; Hurst, Allot.

Huddersfield: Bevan, Jenkins, Moses, Schofield (Baldry 80), Irons, Youds, Smith, Sharp (Stead 46), Brown, Worthington (Thorrington 63), Mattis

Attendance: 4,194

December Report

Well, it was the beginning of December and I was over a third of the way through the season and I had seen 8 matches. The clubs were suffering the varying peaks and troughs that football throws at you.

Derby County was now lower mid table. Probably safe from relegation due to some even more appalling teams than they were, they were in that strange position where everyone said that "Just a few wins and we could get into the playoffs". I like the play-offs but a downside is that teams that have no chance of finishing third or fourth try to convince their supporters and perhaps the players, that they can reach sixth or seventh. This despite the fact the reason that they are mid table is that they are not good enough to get promotion and will not get that good run because they are not good enough as witnessed by their mediocre results. The Rams could get an occasional win but then trip up against poor teams such as Brighton.

Off the field things looked bleak. Various experienced players had their contracts paid up. Carbonari and O'Neil were two, and Ravanelli could join them since he was virtually ruled out for the rest of the season. Poom had been loaned out to Sunderland and would probably be sold when the transfer window reopened. The remaining players were likely to be asked to take a pay cut. Supporters had set up a Rams Trust, which had a big launch at the Assembly Rooms last Friday, but whether Lionel Pickering, owner of the club, would let them have much influence was too early to say.

Things looked brighter in the Derbyshire League, also known as the Unibond First division, where Alfreton, Belper and Matlock were all in the top four. Alfreton were storming into a nine point lead, beaten just once in the league all season. The G-Force were doing the business, with

Godber on 25 goals and Goddard, now out with a hernia on 10.

Borrowash however were still rooted to the bottom of the NCE Premier Division. Shirebrook, Long Eaton and Mickleover had a chance of replacing them being in 2nd, 3rd and 4th spots in Division One. Shirebrook and Mickleover were still in the FA Vase so chance of national glory still remained for now...

Sportscene Talk-In
BBC Radio Derby
Monday 9th December 2002

It is strange to think that there was a time before football phone-ins. Last January Sportscene Talk-in had its 12th birthday and claimed that they were the first. Back in the 1980's of course there was very little football on TV either. We were restricted to an occasional Sunday afternoon live match on ITV presented by Elton Welsby, and Saint and Greavesy on Saturday lunchtime.

Then 606 burst onto the scene (I wasn't in the Radio Derby broadcast area so I cannot comment on its claims) in 1992 and it boomed overnight. Without mass media campaigns it spread by word of mouth between football fans and passed on through the pages of the relatively new fanzines. Most people were sceptical at first when they were told about this brilliant programme, after all it was a new concept, but then the next time you saw them they would be excitedly talking about Danny Baker's ideas and views.

Previously football programmes just reflected the establishment. You could not imagine Ian St John calling for chairmen to resign, or telling the FA they were out or order. If Bob Wilson was chatting to someone he would be unlikely to cut them off mid sentence when they started trying to defend the indefensible. Yet here was a programme where fans could say what they truly thought. Chairmen, directors and officials were banned from appearing. As well as fans calling in to vent their frustrations or sing praises, Danny always called for stories on certain subjects. These included the strangest player's name, the dullest match and 'have you ever gone to the wrong ground'? It was his show and he would cut people off if necessary, such as when an Arsenal fan (who never went to Highbury) tried to defend the Arsenal Bond.

Admittedly some of what he said was over the top, especially in regard to referees.

The following season other stations and Sky made their own versions. A few months later Danny Baker left the show. Eventually he was 'replaced' by David Mellor. Most people I knew stopped listening as he tore up the format and started fawning up to the big clubs, letting directors call in and generally ruining the show in a way that should have been a criminal offence.

Phone-ins have survived, with everyone seemingly having them at least once a week. Moving with the times you can now e-mail and text as well as phone. Radio Derby's is on a Monday evening 6:00-7:00. It is presented by Colin Gibson with regular pundit/expert Ian Hall, a former Derby County player.

Today, like many previous programmes, the talk was not on the latest formation, tactics and the quality of particular players. Instead it was dominated by the financial crisis at the club. The first caller summed up the next hour as he complained at being kept in the dark and asking who was in charge. As well the recycling of old news there was recent surprise that Craig Burley had not been paid since September and had been unable to find the directors to discuss it. Chairman and owner Lionel Pickering was very quiet and wherever there is a void in football (and even where there is not) rumours grow like some evil plant life in a science fiction film.

Chris from Chellaston said it was a fiasco and a farce. He and many others feared what would happen when the transfer window reopened, and it was easy to understand why. The Rams had been told to raise money, but the financial climate had changed beyond all recognition in the past year with transfer fees and players values dropping faster than Marconi shares. Lionel Pickering had allegedly refused to sell Poom in the summer for over £4 million, but now were loaning him to Sunderland in the hope of getting

£2.5 million for him. Dion Burton, a useful first division player, was about to be sold to table topping Portsmouth for less than £250,000, a fee that not so long ago would have got you a reserve player from the 3rd division.

Colin and Ian had no answers, only more questions. How many would be left in February? What would happen if Derby were on the fringe of the playoffs (stop laughing at the back)? Would they risk trying to hang on to players or sign short term deals to attempt to get promotion? Although it was probably depressing to Derby fans, phone-ins are usually at the most lively after defeats or when there is a crisis. Last season the presenters noted that more people telephoned after a defeat than after a win, although that might have been because the fans were all stunned that week! When Jim Smith and later Colin Todd were sacked callers to Sportscene Talk-In were restricted to short calls in order to fit everyone in. Similarly I have noticed in the Boro fanzine Fly Me To The Moon is at its most cutting and funny in times of crisis because it is easier to write critical articles slamming players than it is to say everything is OK. After Man Utd started winning everything a fan wrote in a newspaper that their fanzines were becoming stale because there was nothing to have a go about. That would be a problem that I am sure Derby fans would welcome.

Having recently acquired a computer I tuned into Rampage Radio after Sportscene ended. Rampage was Derby County's very own radio station, available only on the internet and via satellite TV. Programming was limited to a breakfast show, a drive time show, and match commentary. The rest of the time they played music controlled by a computer, which makes you wonder what musical taste pc's have. The audience was especially limited considering that more people listen to the radio in the car or on a Walkman rather than through their TV or pc.

The idea of a club radio station intrigued me. Some have had their own TV station for a while (incidentally Boro

TV being the first, beating MUTV by a year) but radio is quite new. At a Pride Park open day the studio was included in the tour and I asked a presenter whether they thought they were competing with Radio Derby. He was a bit hesitant to answer, but said that he hoped that all Derby fans would listen first and foremost to the club's station, as it was their station. It would be another way that they could show their support. If that began to happen I wonder what Radio Derby would do. Would they tone down their sport output? Would that in turn lead to very little on other stations where new potential fans listened? On Teesside many people who do not go to the games know exactly what's going on via sports news on local radio. However my scenario is admittedly rather hypothetical and far-fetched.

My other question was how free was the station to say what they thought. On Sportscene Talk-in there had been a number of passionate opinions by the presenters as well as the callers, in which they demanded action to be taken. Would Derby County employees be that free? How would Lionel Pickering feel if people criticised his decisions on a radio station that he in effect owned? Mr. Radioman again paused as he wondered how to answer. He hoped that people would be able to express themselves, and but they were all Derby supporters so they all wanted to get behind the club. This seemed rather optimistic if not naive.

Today I was hoping to listen to Black and White Balls, the fans phone-in with Roger Davies. Roger is described on the leaflet I had as a Derby legend, but although I had heard of a fair number of former players I had to look up to find who he was. In case you don't know either (although if you are a Rams fans you should be ashamed, as at least I have a good excuse for my ignorance!) he was a striker in the 1970's and part of the second championship winning team. This was all irrelevant since it was not on and there was Keith with Drivetime instead. What had happened I don't know. I e-mailed the studio to ask them but got no reply. The pc can obviously pick records but can't e-mail.

Burton Albion v Dagenham & Redbridge
Eton Park
Nationwide Conference
Saturday 21st December 2002

Some of you may be a little puzzled. No, not by the fact that this book was ever published, but by my inclusion of Burton. Burton after all is not in Derbyshire. However it seemed to be Derbyshire, with the club second only to Derby in coverage on Radio Derby and in the Derby Evening Telegraph and a number of books in Derby Local Studies feature Derby and Burton together. Neither is Burton in Wales. Before you think I have got the geographical knowledge of a geography graduate (who never seem to know where anywhere is) a former girlfriend who was born and bred in Burton passionately claimed that she was as Welsh as Owain Glyn Dwr.

I hope Burtonians are not too upset by my comments. They are right on the border, on the other side of the Trent, but that is massive psychological gap. A glance at various websites will show that Burton and Gresley Rovers supporters refer to each other as 'the lot over the river'. These differences may seem parochial to outsiders, but to those involved everything takes on immense significance as they argue who has the best team and whose women are the most attractive. Derbies between the two, although rare, are the key fixtures of the season.

When I arrived in Burton I did not see any massed male voice choirs or anything stereotypically Derbyshireish. I didn't see much at all through the gloom and mist, but perhaps on the Saturday before Christmas they had gone shopping instead. Christmas affects the football world in a strange way. Reporters and commentators find it obligatory to squeeze in every reference imaginable as defences are Scrooge-like, goalkeepers provide Christmas presents for the opposition, and Christmas comes early, if it is before the 25th, for goalscorers. The programme of fixtures means that it is crucial time with 12 points up for grabs in 12 days or less, with the accompanying tradition of shock results. Every manager will be repeating the mantra/cliché that it is a crucial time and that by taking many of those points the season can be saved/resurrected/improved. If your club gets stuffed more often than the turkey and drops faster than the needles on your tree then your problems are intensified.

Boxing Day and New Year's Day matches are often derbies and so make this time even more special. I was amazed to read that for many years matches were also played on Christmas Day itself, and here was I thinking that Christmas Dinner was a tradition that was set in stone. Even with today's football fixtures forcing clubs to play at every time and day conceivable I find it hard to imagine Sky scheduling a game for 25th December nowadays.

The car parks in Burton had been full all day with people shopping but I was pleased to see that there was a reasonable crowd in, some entering into the Christmas spirit by wearing Santa hats. It is a decent ground, brightly painted in the club's yellow and black. Importantly it was mostly under cover. I decided to watch from the Popside Terrace by the side of the pitch. In the programme notes manager Nigel Clough respected the aforementioned tradition by insisting that Christmas was an important time and that a good run was needed.

Getting the pre-match atmosphere going was the mascot Billy Brewer. Burton was historically known for the brewing industry and it gave the team their nickname. It just seems a little strange that the kiddies' mascot is a brewer and the junior supporters clubs is called Junior Brewers. What does the local health authority think? Do the eight-year-olds get taught the secret of a good bitter or which hops are the best to use? Lack of time and interest will prevent me from investigating this further.

It soon transpired that Dagenham were the better side. They were better able to retain possession and create chances, whilst Burton were restricted to half chances. A long spell of possession round the penalty area was only ended when they sportingly headed the ball out of the ground. Dagenham's Fletcher brushed Glenn Kirkwood aside before hitting the ball wide with just the goalie to beat.

I had seen Kirkwood last season playing and scoring for Ilkeston. He was a striker then but here he was a makeshift defender, which I don't think on this evidence will be repeated too often. Other Brewers had Derbyshire connection too (not that I'm desperately looking) with goalkeeper Matt Duke having played for Matlock, Blount came from Gresley Rovers, striker Christian Moore had also been a star forward at Ilkeston and squad members Garner, Wassell and Kavanagh were ex-Rams.

Duke was to prove to be the game's key player. When Burton's Darren Stride headed the ball at goal in a rare Brewers attack, the ball went back straight through their midfield and defence. Duke managed to get a hand to the ball when one on one with the outstanding Junior McDougald, before scrambling across the box to punch the ball clear when opponents bore down on the goal. Minutes later he managed to push a free kick round for a corner to deny a goal again.

There were occasional chances for Burton, Dudley almost beat the Daggers goalie to a long ball, but the half was summed up by Burton's first corner (in the 31st minute) when they needed a defender kicking the ball onto his own goal line to give them a shot on target.

As soon as first half ended I headed for the refreshment kiosk to try a faggot. For the uninitiated, as I had been, this is a ball of spicy meat in gravy and Burton claim to be the only club in Britain to serve it. I normally don't eat food at

63

football grounds, partly due to exorbitant costs (although some clubs seem very reasonable) and an experience on a freezing cold night many years ago when I thought I might have a pie to warm me up, only to find that the pie was colder than the sub zero air temperature. I may be tempted to change my opinion because the faggot was pretty good. The downside though was that I found it hard to follow the first quarter of an hour of the second half whilst still queuing.

At least the Brewers laid on half time entertainment, with five adult supporters trying to score the goal from the centre spot for a case of lager (appropriately). The prize was safe though as in the ten minutes none of them even nearly managed it, and embarrassingly neither did the Burton sub goalkeeper who gate-crashed the competition.

The second half was similar to the first as the Brewers spent most of the time chasing the ball and in last ditch defending. Although they struggled to live with the lively Dagenham strikers they at least kept battling away and managed to get a foot in when needed or crowd out McDougald and friends. Nigel Clough was perhaps wondering whether to make any changes to reorganise his troops to compete with Dagenham. Dale Anderson was brought on as a second striker but they still barely threatened to score.

Clough was a brave man to go into management since he would forever be compared with his father. There is a story that Richard Hutton was told for the umpteenth time that he was not as good cricketer as his father, England's Sir Len. Richard correctly pointed out that he had taken more wickets than his batsman Dad, which usually took his critics by surprise. Nigel had obviously taken notice of his Dad's path to glory and started at the bottom, coincidentally or not at the team that his Godfather Peter Taylor began at.

The legend of Brian Clough casts a shadow over football but especially in Derby. With Taylor he took a mediocre second division team and won a League

Championship with them and got to the semi-finals of the European Cup. He left at the height of his popularity (with supporters anyway) which means that his time will always be considered a golden age. When he launched his latest book a few months back there were long queues at every book-signing showing that his legend is still intact.

There are a host of stories about him, most probably untrue but we want them to be because they are the no nonsense ideology that we want to admire. Whilst Colin Todd was briefly Rams manager he went on Sportscene Talk In. A fan rang to tell how to turn things around, in case it hadn't occurred to Colin. He said that in a bad run Cloughie got the players training morning, noon and night and told the players if they didn't start winning this would continue. Colin Todd politely told the caller that he had played under Brian Clough and that had never happened. Another myth bites the dust.

Back on the pitch Brewers goalkeeper Matt Duke deserved the Victoria Cross and any other honour you care to mention for his performance. He pushed an effort into the side netting, dropped on the ball when a striker was about to shoot and saved a shot from point blank range. In between he received a yellow card when he fouled McDougald after racing outside his area. Defenders played their part too with crucial goal line clearances. It is games like these that make you glad than teams can draw. Although the Daggers were the better side I felt that Burton surely needed some reward for their effort and still had something to cling to.

The writing was surely on the wall on 83 minutes when the visitors got into the box and supplied the perfect cross for skipper Matthews on the edge of the 6-yard box. What followed would have made Ronnie Rosenthal blush as he managed to volley it over the bar when it was easier to score. Yes, it is not a cliché it really was easier to score from my vantage point. It was what is technically called a centre-back's shot, which shouldn't be surprising since he is a centre-back. With the weather getting mistier by the minute Burton hung on for an unlikely point.

Burton would have to improve if they were to make progress up the table and look to get into the Football League. Although it was probably a dream at the moment League football has been seen in Burton before. Incredibly for a number of years Burton had two, that's right two teams in the League at a time when there were only two divisions. The Swifts and Wanderers didn't make much impact, and were merged to form Burton United in 1901 but they dropped out the league six years later. Albion date from 1950 and have gradually climbed the pyramid. For a number of years they were just short of getting promotion to the Conference before Clough finally led them to the promised lands of the Conference.

Burton Albion 0 – 0 Dagenham & Redbridge

Burton: Duke; Henshaw, Kirkwood, Reddington (Blount 73), Webster; Dudley (Anderson 68), Glasser, Stride, Burns, Talbot, Moore

D&R: Roberts, Smith, Potts, Matthews, Vickers, Rooney, Terry, Shipp, McGrath, McDougald, Fletcher

Att: 1,447

Matlock Town v Bishop Auckland
Causeway Lane
Northern Premier (Unibond) League Division One
Saturday 4th January 2003

It had reached that stage in the winter when one eye was constantly kept on the weather forecast to see if the matches were still on. The threat this week was rain as hundreds of flood warnings were delivered by the Met Office. It hit home to me how much rain we'd had on New Year's Day. A walk at Dale Abbey with friends from church wasn't so much a walk as a squelch as the paths were pure mud. Not that this bothered us. There's nothing quite like going through mud, provided you don't fall over of course.

By the time Saturday arrived the concern had changed to frost and snow. I woke up to see a hard frost outside. It looked a lovely morning though as I went to work, with a bright blue cloudless sky, but the state of the Causeway Lane pitch was in the back of my mind.

In my first winter in Derbyshire we had only had a very brief covering of snow, and so far this winter we had only had a slight cold snap. When I had moved I had been told stories about villages being cut off for weeks on end and apocryphal tales of mobile libraries getting stuck in the snow, although admittedly it was probably the High Peak they were meaning. Whilst I am not looking for long spells of Arctic weather there is something appealing about the snow. The novelty of a sudden snowfall still brings out the child. Yes I know after a couple of days it loses the said novelty but I can't help it.

The feeling may be partly due to growing up in Thornaby-on-Tees. We must have had the least amount of snowfall in the country. Snow could be a foot deep a few miles out and the moors road to Whitby closed off, but in Thornaby there would be nothing. It was not uncommon to see teachers arriving with snow piled on their roofs whilst we didn't even have a hint of a snowflake. Mentioning school reminds me that snow appears to increase the chances of the school heating failing and therefore being sent home early, which was another advantage.

Today I was pleased to see that the weather had not been too severe and late morning the match was declared on. Driving up it looked quite picturesque with the touch of frost on the fields and hills. Matlock is virtually the centre of Derbyshire both geographically and politically, since this is where the County Council has its HQ. Matlock is actually made up various Matlocks including Matlock Bath and Matlock Bank. The Matlocks came to prominence in the early 19th century when the upper classes travelled here to take the waters. Hydrotherapy continued into the twentieth century but before you book your visit I'm afraid that there are no spas are left.

This season with going well as the football club alternated between third and fourth with Derwent Valley rivals Belper Town. Just a few miles away Alfreton were running away with the league. However the supporters were not getting carried away with anything. When I asked the programme seller how the season was going he said OK, and when he checked and saw they were third he couldn't believe it. He was almost as surprised as the Heanor fans were when they discovered their team was higher up the table than they'd thought. I'd also noticed some discontent on the website forum as criticism was directed at the committee. Concern was expressed about ambition, management, tactics and team spirit; although as one person pointed out things can't be too bad if you are third in the table. It was also not too dissimilar to what I had read on other club's forums. Where would football supporters be without something to moan at?

As I took my position near the halfway line I asked my neighbour how Matlock were playing. "We've just had two

68

nil-nils and we didn't score the match before either", he explained. Perhaps I'd chosen the wrong match. Perhaps not, since the Gladiators created three good chances in the opening few minutes. Bishop Auckland didn't help themselves when the goalkeeper let a through ball go through his legs on the edge of the area but by the time striker Steve Taylor had run past and got a shot in a defender had got back to block it.

On 15 minutes Matlock took the lead. A left wing cross was knocked down by Varley and Danny Holland scored from a few yards out. The teenager was the player 'Captain Gladiator' had told me to look out for when I went onto Matlock's website forum, and he was living up to the praise. The home supporters seemed more relieved than happy at the goal, but they didn't have long to savour it as Bishop Auckland stormed back by forcing Kevin Tye to push a free kick over for a corner, and soon after Jonathan Mann got goal side of his marker and scored from an angle into the far corner of the net.

But Matlock aren't nicknamed the Gladiators for nothing, and they raised their game. Ex-Chesterfield striker Taylor crossed from the left but this time Varley didn't need anyone as he nodded the ball down from almost under the crossbar. A minute later they forced a corner, and it looked like a third had been scored when the visiting goalkeeper, Caffrey, did an impression of a man in a shower grabbing for the soap as the ball squirmed out of his grip and over the line. At least the referee spared his blushes and awarded a fortuitous free kick.

Matlock continued to press forward and Taylor ran into the penalty area, shrugged off the defender and scored goal number three and his fifteenth of the season. Four goals in eight minutes was more than I could hope for, and it left me wondering what the final scoreline would be. There were 65 minutes left, and eight went into 65 just over eight times, and multiplied by four made 32. Yes, I know it was unrealistic but this conversation goes on at every match whenever there is a spate of goals, booking or other incidents.

A young couple went past for a third time with a bucket. The sign on the said bucket said "New Stand Fund" so I put a pound in. Their quiet approach that could almost go unnoticed was the opposite of Mr Raffleman's technique at Mickleover. However I was persuaded to donate today, whilst I'd managed to avoid this at Station Road so there must be something to be said for not speaking.

Causeway Lane could do with some improvements, and even the club admits this. The stand behind me only had a section open and the rest seemed to be storing loose chairs and other junk. Opposite was the main stand which had seen better days, to my left was a covered terrace of sorts and behind the other goal was the cricket pitch. To avoid demotion Matlock would need to enclose the cricket pitch side, lay tarmac round the perimeter, improves the players' tunnel area and install new showers, all before March 31. The committee had this in hand and announced that Tarmac was supplying the tarmac and Paul Plumbing was installing the showers. I kid you not.

The crowd seemed reasonable for non-league (it turned out to be 277) although everyone was spread out round most of the perimeter. Just over 25 years ago over 5,000 packed in to Causeway Lane twice as Matlock had their greatest period. In the 1960's they rose up through the leagues winning the Central Alliance League and Midlands Counties League. Under the management of ex-Sheffield Wednesday and England defender Peter Swan they reached the first round of the FA Cup in 1975, losing to Blackburn Rovers, before meeting Scarborough at Wembley in the FA Trophy Final. Before a 20,000 crowd (including the Duke of Devonshire) they won 4-0 on the greatest day in their history. They returned to a heroes' welcome and within the week had added their first Derbyshire Senior Cup to their collection.

The next season continued in this successful vein as under new manager Tom Fenoughty they beat Mansfield to get to the FA Cup third round and finished as runners up in the Northern Premier League. By these standards the Derbyshire Senior Cup, NPL Shield and NPL Cup wins barely merit a mention. These successes did allow Matlock to qualify for Europe, in the shape of the Anglo-Italian Non-league Cup. Younger readers should note that this was not the short lived 1990's competition which saw Derby playing Cremonese in the final at Wembley, and memorable for the vast number of red cards shown in the group games as Anglo-Italian relations were strained to the limit. Although both away matches were lost Matlock beat both Juniorcasale and, coincidently, Cremonese at home 2-0 and even appeared live on cable TV. Yes, that's right, cable TV in the 1970's.

Unsurprisingly they couldn't maintain this record and silverware had been harder to come by in recent decades. Six seasons ago they were relegated from the Premier League into the Division One and a solitary Derbyshire Senior Cup was the only success in the 1990's.

Back on the field of play Matlock dominated. Left back Steve Charles, a sprightly 42 year old, came closest to getting number four when his header clipped the post. Bishop Auckland struggled to create chances as McNicholas, Lukic and captain Chris James stood firm. Lukic in particular stood out with some great tackles.

At half time I wandered over to the tea hut for a soup to warm me up and a sausage cob. The sun had gone and the temperature was dropping.

The second half began at a furious pace and both teams attacked but there were few shots of note. John Caffrey in the Bishops goal continued to look decidedly dodgy and rarely looked comfortable, but was not tested too much.

Half way through the half Matlock stepped up a gear and threatened to score as they dominated. Taylor's shot to the near post was pushed away for a corner and then Lukic on a forage forward played a one-two with Brown before his shot in turn was deflected. From the resulting corner Brown hit the crossbar with Caffrey not knowing what to do. Surely Bishop Auckland couldn't continue to hold out, and on 75 minutes they literally gave Matlock a helping hand by handling the ball in their box. The referee waved play on but the linesman had spotted it. Lukic took responsibility for the kick and coolly hit it into the bottom left hand corner. In case you are wondering, John Lukic is his uncle.

Most of the Bishops seemed to give up at this point. Steve Taylor seemed to be enjoying himself as he ran rings around the right back. The exception was their number 11 who kept trying right till the end, and was reward for hard work by scoring a consolation goal from the edge of the area. A minute later he almost made it 4-3.

I was quite pleased to see them get a goal back. I had better stress that I wanted Matlock to win, but I still had some fascination with Bishop Auckland. They are almost legendary in non-league football, winning the Northern League 18 times and the FA Amateur Cup ten times. Their light blue and dark blue halved shirts (not worn today due to the blue shirts of the home team) were distinctive. However despite only living a few miles from them for many years I had never bothered going to see them. The only time I had been to the town was when I briefly worked in the Bishop Auckland Hospital's medical library for a few weeks. A fortnight there was long enough to learn never to look inside a dermatology magazine if you want to eat within the next few hours.

The three points meant that they reduced the gap with second placed North Ferriby to three points. I walked back to my car, avoiding the temptation of the signposted lido. During the match it was cold, but now I was moving it seemed to penetrate my entire body. I still had to defrost my car, and I wondered once more whether my car was the only one in the world that got more ice on the inside of the windows than the outside. My fingers stopped stinging as I drove through Matlock Bath and I began to get proper feeling again by the time I reached Belper.

Matlock Town 4 – 2 Bishop Auckland
Holland 15, Varley 20   Mann 17
Taylor 23, Lukic (P) 75   Irvine 90

Matlock: Tye, James, Charles (Hollinsworth 84), Clarke, McNicholas, Lukic, Varley (Handbury 87), Brown (Tilley 80), Taylor, Holland, Williams

Bishop Auckland: Caffrey, Lydon, Smith, Leadbitter, Moss, Hope, Ross (O'Riordan 80), Salvin, Mann, Cowie (Maddison 87), Irvine

Att: 277

Gresley Rovers v Redditch United
The Moat Ground
Southern (Dr Martens) League Western Division
Saturday 26th January 2003

How do you feel about progress? Do you look back on the past as a golden age that isn't a patch on today's world? Or do you throw yourself into every change that today brings and just have to subscribe to every innovation? I hope I take a balanced view, valuing our heritage whilst remembering that it should not constrict our lives today. Sometimes though people, and it is always other people of course because I am too level headed, get carried away with technology. I've seen people get irate at being asked to turn a mobile phone off in a cinema or train because they absolutely must be able to receive a call in the next few minutes or else the world will explode. There have also been people who think that civilisation has broken down because their dishwasher broke down and it cannot be repaired for a few hours.

My vice is the Internet. How did we manage before it? No, honestly, how did we manage? Today I send numerous e-mails at work, corresponding with colleagues all over Derby and beyond at a flick of a mouse. Whenever the network goes down I'm stuck. When I was at university in Aberystwyth everyone communicated via e-mail, organising social events and other things, and you always checked before going out in case there was a message telling you of alternative arrangements. Whilst studying in Dudley just two years or so earlier we didn't use it at all, yet we still got on with life.

The web is a phenomenon. This season I have been keeping up to date with many of Derbyshire's football clubs via their websites. Clubs with a hundred supporters have vast sites containing everything you want to know about the club, with match reports, histories, player databases and discussion boards. Some of them are official sites, such as Alfreton, others are fan based, and Ilkeston even have two unofficial ones as well the club's own site. Where else could I have found this mine of information? Nowhere.

Fan forums give supporters the opportunity to communicate. I love debates amongst real football supporters, as they debate and share their pain. As I've eavesdropped, though, I have also seen others come on with trollish behaviour. I use this word because I found out this week that a troll on the internet is someone who deliberately causes trouble. People from other clubs sometimes invade other forums and resort to the, "you lot stink, na-na-na-na-na-na", argument, which whilst is good enough for politicians does not really encourage in depth analysis.

Many of these are created and kept going by an enthusiastic volunteer, that wondrous creature of non-league football. In some cases it is phenomenal, with the Football Club History Database an example. In this site they have each season's records for hundreds if not thousands of football clubs. Right down to Ashbourne United, Graham Street Prims and Mickleover Royal British Legion you can see their record for each year. It is a site I have visited weekly.

Gresley's website is amongst the best, featuring a comprehensive history, a database of players going back 50 years or more, match reports and photos. Just as importantly it is up to date. The latest development is a latest score facility that, strangely enough, gives the latest score. Yes, that means that someone in Outer Mongolia can, if they are hooked up to the Information Superhighway, know within minutes when Gresley have scored. They also have a discussion board, on which I placed a request for a Gresley fan's view of the club. Despite 50 people looking at my message they decided to steer clear of the weird Boro fan in their midst, since no one did reply, and who can blame them.

Whatever the website and technology is like, the place where things really matter is on the football field. As I took up my position on the terrace opposite the main stand, I asked the chap next to me, wearing a purple shirt, how Rovers were playing this season. "We're pretty consistent in the fact that we are inconsistent", he told me. I think I knew what he meant.

Both sides made an edgy start. Gresley had the first chance when Andy Bourne and the Redditch goalie both went for a 50:50 ball from a free kick but the keeper just grabbed it in time. A few minutes later his opposite number was called into action but couldn't catch a low cross. A mad scramble ensued as he flung himself to knock the ball away from the posse of visiting players. "Stop breakdancing" one of my neighbours shouted out. Lindley had obviously not won over the fans in the two years since he moved from Notts County. "He's a decent shot stopper, but if there is anything more complicated you're in trouble", was the considered opinion around me.

After quarter of an hour a ball was played into the Redditch penalty area for Slater to chase, but it was over hit. Goalkeeper Anstiss didn't realise that the danger was over and obligingly pulled Carl Slater down. It was a clear penalty, but even the home fans realised that it was pretty fortunate, "Top bombing" being the opinion of Mr Purpleshirt. Mark Peters took responsibility for the kick, but his shot was a metre off the ground, the ideal height for Anstiss to redeem himself and push round for a corner.

The game then settled down with few clear chances created. Redditch were a competent side with some physically strong players that Gresley found hard to get past. However Redditch struggled to create any clear opening and despite the occasional wobble by Lindley they never really looked like scoring. Rovers had to rely on

Redditch gifts for opportunities, Kitching intercepting a back pass before losing the ball before he could shoot, and then Bourne receiving a pass from Anstiss but he couldn't capitalise either.

An interesting battle on the pitch was between Redditch midfielder Taylor and Gresley's youngster Carl Timms, a mismatch in terms of height and bulk. It looked pitiable when Taylor outmuscled Timms without breaking stride for the second or third time, but Timms just picked himself up, chased back and then won the ball with an amazing tackle.

At left back for Rovers was Gary White, who had played for Crewe reserves during the week. He looked fairly good, and therefore stood out today. He looked solid at the back, making some crunching tackles that kept the visiting physio on his toes. Going forward he looked to have that little bit extra too, and seemed to be involved whenever Gresley threatened. However he was not immune from mistakes and Mr Purpleshirt was worried in case the potential transfer fee was cut with every misplaced pass. It was one of these, a free kick straight into touch, that ended the first half, and it probably summed up the match so far.

Gresley are a club that has risen throughout the past 50 years, going from 1959 to 1999 without relegation as they progressed from the Birmingham League Division Two to the Southern League Premier Division, not bad for a small mining village in South Derbyshire. Silverware flowed into the Moat Ground cabinet in unprecedented numbers, as various league championships and cups were won, including seven Derbyshire Senior Cup wins in ten years. One highlight in all this was reaching the FA Vase final at Wembley, which they drew 4-4 only to lose in a replay.

If it wasn't for the standard of their ground they could even have reached the Conference and who knows what would have happened. Under Paul Futcher they won the Southern League, but were denied promotion. I was intrigued to see Futcher's name, since my only knowledge of his management career was at Darlington, where he seemed as suited to management as Bryan Robson. Here he became notorious as the manager who couldn't win. For all everyone's protestations that he was popular with the players and was doing a great job, two points and three goals in ten games sealed his fate. I had assumed that he would have sought out a new career, but you have to admire him for sticking at it, and admire Gresley for giving him a job despite this record.

The current incumbent was Jon Newsome. I'm sorry to say that I knew little about him, which is embarrassing considering he has a League Championship medal to his name won just ten years ago. This was from his time with Leeds. Cantana, Lukic, Strachan, Chapman and Whyte spring to mind, but I can't recall Newsome. If you are reading this, sorry!

Reminiscing was a good idea because the second half was as bad as the first. It could have been different if Kitching or any other Gresley player managed not to miss a good cross that appeared to be just right. Bourne managed to completely miss a cross to him a few minutes later too. At the other end Lindley did well to get a touch on a long-range shot, and when the impressive Hill hit a shot soon after, Lindley managed to fall on the ball and save it.

The defining moment came on the hour, when Gresley got the ball into the box and had a number of chances as Redditch struggled to clear, but they all went begging. Mr Purpleshirt had run a bit further up the terrace in anticipation of a goal, and flung his arms about in frustration. Everyone was now convinced, even with 30 minutes to go, that they were not going to score today. Ten minutes later it was no surprise when Bourne hit the ball out of the ground when he was given a chance in the area.

The Moat Ground is tightly packed into a housing estate, the sort where it has to be one way systems because roads are so narrow. The boundary wall is only a couple of metres from the pitch edge so tall netting is placed on top. It only took five minutes for the first ball to disappear from view as Rovers captain Evans booted the ball into a garden. Players from both sides seemed to accept the challenge of repeating this at every given opportunity, and to do this when you are just a few yards in front of an open goal must be some achievement that not even Diego Forlan could repeat. Mr Purpleshirt told me that they never lost any balls, and he pointed out strategically placed ladders for the ball boys to climb over into the gardens. "Mind", he said, "it's a little worrying when they return with video recorders, gnomes and bikes under their arms."

As the game stuttered towards the finish Redditch managed to get a few chances and show why they were a couple of places above Gresley. Wardle, who had been with Gresley for 12 years, kicked the ball off the line. Ian Bluck then made a brilliant tackle on Hill. Quiggan, another visiting striker, impressed everyone when he hurdled an outstretched leg in the penalty area as he vainly chased a long through ball. Many would have gone down and it would have been a certain penalty, but credit to him for resisting temptation and trying to play on.

At the end Gresley had a bit of possession, but there was little chance of a late winner. By now they seemed unable to get the ball into the box. White summed it up when he went on a good run, but when he got to the area he stopped as if he didn't know what to do. I asked around me if they usually played better than this. One man said yes, but Mr Purpleshirt thought not much better. It would be hard to imagine a worse performance. It seemed a blessing when the whistle blew.

Gresley Rovers 0 v 0 Redditch United

Gresley: Lindley, Moran, White, Bluck, Evans (Wardle 25), Cheetham, Timms, Peters, Bourne, Kitching (Barrett 51), Slater. Sub (not used) Newsome, Hopkins, B Smith.

Redditch: Anstiss, Manton, Townsend, Taylor, Knight, Shaw (Clarke 64), Field, Cowley, Quiggan (Hill 85), Rowell (Arshad 45), Hall

Attendance: 378

Graham Street Prims v Greenwood Meadows
Asterdale
Central Midlands Football League - Supreme Division
Saturday 1st February 2003

Why? It is a question that sometimes has no answer that we can put down in words. Why do we do what we do? Why do we like what we like? A friend once said that it would be fun to visit every Woolworth's in the country. I gave him a puzzled look as I asked him why. He retorted why do people climb Everest, or row across the Atlantic? I myself have had trouble answering the question. When I went for a job interview in Barnstaple a few years ago I was asked why I wanted the job. I was a bit concerned that I hadn't explained it adequately when I was asked it six times.

Just why people put in the time and effort with small non-league clubs could mystify many. Constant work just to keep things going, with seemingly very little in return, but I'm really glad they do it. Graham Street Prims are a good example of a club that attracts these people. I first met Dave Tice, General Manager, in the library a couple of months ago when he was researching the club's history. He is at the ground before matches, preparing the ground, and then clearing away at the end. Most Tuesdays he and a group of supporters spend a few hours doing odd jobs, and if there is a match then they can spend ten hours there. He pointed out a few men to me who had been associated with Prims for 50 years.

The strange name is due to their origins at Primitive Methodist Chapel in Graham Street. If you look on a modern map, as I did, you won't find Graham Street anywhere due to its demolition in the 1960's. I eventually located it in Osmaston just a couple of goal kicks away from the Baseball Ground. They began in 1904, hence Dave's timely efforts to trace the beginnings, but they disbanded in 1914 as did many other clubs. This was not before they produced league players such as the Keetley brothers, and even an England international in Jimmy Bagshaw.

They were reformed in the early 1950's, and some of those involved today began as players then. "We were mostly 15 year olds", the Gateman told me, "but the league said you had to be 16 to play, so we just played friendlies in the first year." Although they were never amongst the top Derbyshire sides they were still successful, winning 15 pieces of silverware between 1971 and 1981. Times got tough though and they merged with Carriage and Wagon in 1995. Repeated vandalism at their ground led to them moving to the Asterdale, home to Borrowash Victoria too, in 1999. Since then they have turned a bit of land into a ground and a table tennis hut into dressing rooms and hospitality area.

Last week at Gresley there wouldn't have been a goal even if we had played all week. Today the opener came in just minutes when Grant squared the ball to McCaul who scored from just inside the penalty box. Minutes later Deakin finished off a good passing move by hitting the ball in off the underside of the cross bar. What do they say about buses coming in pairs?

Prims desperately needed the points against fellow strugglers Greenwood Meadows in order to get themselves out of the bottom three of the Central Midlands League Supreme Division, otherwise they would be relegated to the Premier Division. It takes a while to work out league names and what division trumps another. What happened to the good old days when the top division was the first division? Titles like premier, super, supreme and premiership can be used almost at random. I just wonder what they will use in the future. The Best Division, the Primary League or the Cardinal Competition?

Dropping into the Premiership was looking less likely as the home side kept up the pressure. With plenty of space for anyone who wanted to use it, Prims put in some dangerous balls that had to be hastily cleared or kicked away for corners. Halfway though the half (or quarter of the way though the match if you like) a long ball was played forward for Scott Blaney to chase. The Greenwood goalie looked slightly more likely to get there first, but Blaney didn't bottle it, as a chap near me put it, and stuck out a boot to knock it past the keeper and it trickled into the net to make it 3-0.

"Who are you reporting for?" I stopped scribbling to see the Prims manager talking to me. I had been slightly surprised to be told by Mr Gateman that their manager was an international. I know many managers start at the bottom, such as Martin O'Neil at Grantham, but Asterdale must be even further down. Gerry McElhinney had played for Celtic, Bolton plus various other league clubs in addition to his Northern Ireland caps but it didn't seem the right moment to discuss his career choices.

"I'm doing it for myself", I replied, thinking that this was not the time and place either for an in depth discussion about my hare brained idea.

"That's OK", he said, "I thought you were with the Evening Post. They always get things wrong." So apologies to anyone if I have got your name or anything else wrong.

Goals were not going to be in short supply today, since defences were far too respectful. The cultured Alan Hansen once gave the advice, "If it doubt, give it a clout", and both rearguards could benefit from that wisdom. Chris Hudson, Prims No.1 but no relation, made a great save when a Greenwood striker was unmarked. Minutes later though they had got goal back. A right wing cross came in and a defender appeared to stick out a boot and chip it over Hudson. However on the League website it was credited as a goal for Greenwood's Allison. I hope Gerry's not reading this!

The Prims centre forward was dissimilar in physique to many strikers I'd seen this season, looking a little more stockier. However before Leigh Grant finds out where I live and pays me a visit I should point out that this would still be fitter than most non-footballers. It certainly didn't affect his skills; it just made it slightly more surprising as he kept showing glimpses of great ability. Early on he turned a defender and got a good shot in. A bit later it got even better when he received a ball from a Deakin backheel and with his back to goal turned his marker, dribbled past three players and scored. It was a wonderful goal and got the professional seal of approval as the management team went wild.

Both sides had chances as they approached the break but the score remained 4-1. I followed the other spectators to the hut to get out of the cold. I bought a mug of tea. There is something about being given a mug instead of a polystyrene cup, giving you a level of trust rarely found in football. The last time it happened was at Aberystwyth, when the bloke at the kiosk gave me a mug and said, "Just bring it back when you finish".

I missed the first minute of the second half, but was just in time to see a penalty converted to make it 4-2. This signalled a transformation of the Greenwood team. In the first half Prims shaded it, but now Greenwood completely dominated. Evans in particular began to torment the Prims defence. Fortunately for them Greenwood spurned chances and Hudson was fairly solid in goal. I'd seen outstanding goalkeepers and others who were as dependable as that Italian goalie whose name no one can remember, that Manchester United played until he let in that

Le Tissier goal. I am pleased to say my namesake was above average.

The referee now took centre stage. I have so far refused to comment on referees and the crowd's reactions because it would be so repetitive. Mostly the referees have been OK, although at every ground I've visited everyone of course thinks that they are the worst they have ever seen. Last year at the Ilkeston v Chelmsford match an eighty-year-old lady started screaming obscenities and abuse at the referee. "Are you blind? You have just booked the number 6, so send the dirty so and so off. You're useless". Her daughter quietly mentioned that in fact it was number 5 who had committed the foul. Without a shred of irony she shouted, "Are you blind, book him!"

I am also reminded of a talk given by the then top referee Ken Lupton. He showed a video of the Saint & Greavesie show, when they criticised Lupton for disallowing a Tranmere goal. He then rewound it and you could clearly see a push by the striker, yet our loveable duo, who had endless TV replays at their disposal, completely missed it.

I'd been told at half time that he was one of the worst referees. I was sceptical until he held up play for three minutes in the second half, and asked Dibber to move because he was coaching. Dibber is vice-chairman and nothing to do with the coaching side. He was merely shouting from the sidelines like any other fan. What would he do at Pride Park? Would he go into the East stand and shout, "You 500 fans move, you are not allowed to coach. Stop screaming 'shoot'". Just where would it all end? Minutes later Blaney was caught offside but shot just as the whistle went. The referee harshly decided to book him.

This brief interruption hadn't put Greenwood off since Allison scored to bring them within one goal of Prims. "I told them we would lose at half time". Dibber had come round to join us. There was the graveyard sense of humour common to all struggling clubs, as people predicted disaster to avoid being too disappointed when failure came.

Blaney was given a rare chance when he was one on one with the goalie, but he put it wide. His former club was Borrowash Victoria, who were playing just 500m away so presumably it hadn't taken him long to settle into Prims. To the relief of those around me he got his second of the match, but still raised our blood pressure as he first played a one two with the post. He had also had spell with Derby, Walsall and Burton, and he certainly looked a useful player who should get a fair few goals.

"It could be eight all", Dibber commented, and he wasn't far wrong as Greenwood hit the cross bar again. Prims found it hard to clear the ball and whenever they did the midfield couldn't hold on to it, or they just kicked it anywhere. The inevitable happened and with six minutes left Allison got another goal with a looped header over Hudson. It was his second or possibly his hat-trick. Surely they were not going to lose this? Everyone around me was tense as centre-back Limb made a crucial tackle to stop a shot coming in, and then Hudson made another good block.

Adam Lillie relieved the pressure with a couple of good runs. "He's a promising player and plenty of pace", Dave had told me earlier when he pointed him out to me, "but he's still young and a bit lightweight." This was pretty accurate, not that I doubted what I was told, and the defenders seemed to manage to take the ball off him easily. He did manage to evade them once though, but the shot went wide. He then went on another run. "Go to the corner flag", screamed another Dave. What the referee would have thought of this blatant coaching is anyone's guess but neither he nor Adam heard, and the striker instead went for goal but was tackled. "Youth", everyone muttered, shaking their heads.

The reason they had all these chances was we were having seven minutes of added time. Where it had all come from was anyone's guess, but Dibber and others thought that he was being penalised from earlier and there could be few other explanations. The linesmen had signalled time was up by their reckoning ages ago, but the game flowed merrily along. "My chips are getting cold", someone shouted. "Perhaps we should drop a hint and start taking down the goalnets", Dibber suggested to Dave as another minute elapsed. Hudson managed to save another Greenwood shot, and it seemed that he would have to keep on doing so until the equaliser came. Eventually though the referee decided that any more injury time couldn't be justified and blew for full time. Graham Street Prims were out of the relegation zone.

Graham Street Prims 5 v 4 Greenwood Meadows
McCaul 4, Deakin 7   Allison 28, 70, 84
Blaney 24, 79, Grant 32   Gee 47 (pen)

Graham St Prims: Hudson, Dickenson, Mallon (Lillie), Wollard, Limb, Higgins, McCaul, Hill, Grant (Stevens 76), Blaney, Deakin (Illife 76)

Greenwood: Powell, McDermott, Smith, Warden, Cotton, Ward (Shaw 80), Dean Spencer, Stephens, Allison, Evans, Gee.

Royal Shrovetide Football
Ashbourne
Tuesday 4th March 2003

"It's Pancake Day, it's pancake day, it's p.p.p.p.p. p.p.p.pancake day". This little ditty from Maid Marion & Her Merry Men comes to mind every Shrove Tuesday. Other people think of different things this time of year, whether it be skipping, egg rocking, flamboyant carnivals, being shriven or pancake tossing. The people of Ashbourne think of football. You see this is one of the last bastions of hug football which is a throwback to mass football that anyone can join in and the only rules appear to be that you cannot move the ball by motor vehicle and manslaughter is not per_____ ___. The aim is to strike the ball three times at one of the goals, which are three miles apart.

Exactly when it began is not certain. There is a hint in 1683 although Ashbourne is not mentioned by name but certainly by 1800 it was an established part of Ashbourne life. Some tried to ban this violent custom in the 19th century, and many players were arrested, but thanks to determined Ashburnians it survived. As with many customs, by the very nature of its being traditional was now quaint and something to be treasured. Derby had a game itself between All Saints and St Peter's until it was stopped by the army at the request of the Mayor in the 1840's. As I passed All Saints today, now Derby Cathedral, I noticed that they were having a Quiet Day in preparation for Lent instead.

If I had chosen to go on Ash Wednesday I would have seen Prince Charles getting the match started by turning the ball up, 75 years after a previous Prince of Wales turned up in both senses of the phrase. However this is not why it is called Royal football, since that dated back a few years earlier. George V's daughter Princess Mary was getting

88

married to Lord Lascelles and the good folk of Ashbourne wanted to buy a present. So they headed off to Ranby's in Derby, Debenham's precursor, and looked at the wedding list. They were out of tablecloths, didn't have the right coloured towels and didn't stock the correct design of crockery. Ashbournians scratched their collective heads since the couple already had a dozen toasters and they couldn't think what to buy. Then someone had an idea, "How about sending a Shrovetide football?" "What a good idea", they all exclaimed, "hours of fun for all the family!" So in honour of this wedding gift the game has been called Royal.

In fairness to the people of Ashbourne I should point out that the wedding was taking place on Shrove Tuesday and they did ask first whether Princess Mary would appreciate the ball. I don't suppose she could refuse. Royalty and VIPs seem to be obliged to accept whatever gifts they are offered, whether they are elephants, kangaroos or whatever. Who knows, if it had not been accepted a corner of Derbyshire might have declared itself a republic.

As I wandered round Ashbourne I saw the last minute preparations as joiners were overworked boarding up shops. Many had decided to shut for today and apart from people here for the football the town was quiet making it a good day to sight see. Or it would have been if it hadn't have been overcast and drizzling. It boasts a number of buildings dating back as far as Elizabethan times and it is well worth a visit.

Tradition is an essential ingredient of Royal Shrovetide Football, and part of this is the pre-match meal at the Green Man, consisting of soup, roast beef and Yorkshire puddings, and finishing with apple pie. It makes my mouth water just thinking about it, but I didn't have a ticket. Anyway, I'm sure it wouldn't be up to my Mum's standard. Instead I went for an excellent all day breakfast at Busy Bees Tea Shop. One of the turner upper's duties is to give a speech at the pre-match meal. From what I could gather this was a crucial part of the day and what was said was taken down for posterity. Just what would some Association Football stars make of this? My mind wandered back a few days to an interview David Beckham gave, where in an incisive interview he said that it would be nice to beat Liverpool and win the League Cup. Really David, and here was I thinking that you didn't care about winning and losing and were contemplating playing badly. Although as it turned out...

Refreshed, I headed for Shaw Croft to get a good position for the start. In the car park there was only one brave car. As I waited a couple of other cars, or more accurately the drivers, contemplated coming in to do their shopping, but took one look at the mass rabble and decided that perhaps they didn't need a loaf of bread quite so desperately.

I had been wondering just what it would be like in amongst this crowd. The game has a reputation of being almost like a riot, and part of me wondered if it would be a little intimidating, especially for an outsider such as myself. I don't want to be prejudicial, but seeing pictures of previous games I probably wouldn't want to get on the wrong side of many of the players. However I am probably being extremely unfair. As it turned out the atmosphere was amazing. Most people there were not players but had come to cheer on the teams. Head Teachers are not stupid and ensure that half term always coincides with the matches. The crowd included parents with young children, teenagers rebelliously carrying Red Bull cans, middle aged ex-players and senior citizens.

Today's "turner up" was Bill Hellaby of the Royal British Legion. Before beginning we all sang the traditional songs, Auld Lang Syne and The National Anthem. Seemingly in honour of the occasion the rain had stopped and sun broke through the clouds. A quick reminder was issued to keep out of banned places such as cemeteries, gardens and churchyards, and then we were off. The Up'ards presumably got hold of the ball since the hug headed towards Sturston.

I looked to see where to ball was amongst the mass of bodies, and saw it by spotting the steam rising. By the time I had caught up with the action they had already gone into the Henmore Brook. Water play is a highlight of the game, although I was quite content to watch. Although it can't have been warm today there have been many years when it is barely above freezing. Getting a spot where you could see what was happening appeared to be just as hard as playing the football, since there were a few hundred people crammed round a small part of the brook. The game was at a stalemate for quarter of an hour as neither side could move the hug of players more than a yard or two in either direction.

Suddenly the ball flew out of the hug and landed a few yards away. A mini tidal wave ensued as forty-odd people charged upriver. At this point the 'hard but fair' spirit was suspended as a few fists flew between a couple of players. Whether that distracted the players or not I don't know but someone managed to take the ball out and run away from the brook. I was quite happy to watch from a distance, but I now found myself a few yards from the ball. People around me ran in all directions to try and get out of the way and I was swept along. It wasn't long before the ball came to a halt, and this was the pattern for the next couple of hours as a short burst was made before a period of standing still. This allowed players to come out and take breathers. Whenever it moved sightseers in the way panicked and got out the way as best they could before going back as close as they dared. I suppose it was a rougher version of 'What time is it Mr Wolf?'

Slowly but surely the Up'ards took the ball eastwards towards their goal on a zig-zag line. Ditches and barbed wire fences were minor obstacles to the players. The first part of this went over a normal football pitch. I have no idea who played there but I pity them on Saturday since it now looked like the Somme since hundreds of pairs of feet had churned it up. Every so often the ball would emerge in the air, and we all cheered, before it dropped back into the mass scrum. Just before 4:00 the ball was moved back over the brook. The only way to follow was to wade through and unfortunately I had forgotten to take spare footwear! Since a bus would be leaving soon I thought this would be an appropriate time to take my leave and get back in time for my church's pancake party. Most other spectators called it a day too; many saying that it was time for the pub. As the bus left Ashbourne I looked back. The hug had only got another couple of hundred yards in the half-hour since I'd left.

Next day I discovered that Up'ard Alan Brown had scored at 9:45, with just fifteen minutes to spare. On Ash Wednesday Up'ard Mark Hallam scored with the ball thrown up by Prince Charles. Since it was scored before 6:00 there was time for another ball to be thrown up, the first time this had happened for many years. The Down'ards restored some pride by scoring with this ball. All in all this must be one of the most successful Shrovetides, with mass media coverage accompanying the visit of the Prince of Wales. A photo of a tentative Prince being carried to the plinth on the shoulders of players was on the cover of most newspapers, and there was plenty of TV coverage too. It looked like this tradition was safe for the time being.

Buxton v Harrogate Railway
The Silverlands
Northern Counties East League Premier Division
Saturday 22nd March 2003

In the Buxton clubhouse I chatted to a couple of blokes about how the side were doing this season. "Pretty good", one said, "we score plenty of goals but concede them too." This sounded promising for an entertaining match. "Although we don't have a big squad so when injuries come we are stuck, which is why we are not at the top".

I explained why I was here today. "Well, you picked a good day for it." I certainly had, since the sun was shining and we had a beautiful spring day. I had taken advantage of my trip to spend the morning seeing the town's sites. The crocuses and daffodils were out and even a cynic like me felt good.

Buxton has been a popular destination for almost 2,000 years partly due to their water spring. The bath loving Romans made a settlement here and called it Aquae Arnemetia, Spring of the Goddess of the Grove. In Tudor times many of the nobility came to 'take the waters', including Mary Queen of Scots. This continued over the next couple of centuries as people came for the spa treatments. The decline of spas in the 1920's was compensated for by tourists coming to visit the Peak District.

One of the most distinctive buildings in Buxton is The Crescent, modelled on the one in Bath. At this point I realised that there was only one spa town playing league football, Cheltenham, very recently promoted. Was there a reason why Bath, Buxton, Leamington and Harrogate were still all non-league clubs? Probably not but as wild theories go it is not as weird as some rumours and if I keep repeating it someone may be gullible enough to believe me.

Back in the spa's heyday a law was passed banning poor people from visiting the well to drink the water. I'm pleased to say that when I went to the well nobody asked to see my bank balance. However I had a bit of a wait as people took every container imaginable to collect water to take home. Whether they were taking the government's advice to stock up in case of a terrorism attack or if this was normal I can't say.

Amongst Buxton's other architectural treasures is the Opera House, but I was here for the opera of the people. Yes, I admit that is a corny link. Instead of an elaborate Edwardian building we had Silverlands, with its relatively large main stand and a couple of covered terraced areas. The Bucks claim that it is the highest ground in the country, at 1,000 feet above sea level.

Once inside I headed for the clubhouse, and then sought out Mike Barton, who had responded to my e-mail on the Buxton web forum. "Should be a good game", he told me confidently, "with two in form teams". As programme editor, webmaster, director and general assistant he was another of those unsung servants who non-league clubs rely upon.

Unfortunately for Buxton it was Harrogate who started the stronger once the game began, dominating the first ten minutes play. Backed by a very vocal following they put Buxton's defence under pressure without creating a clear cut chance. Buxton were reduced to long balls forward for the front two of Caine Cheetham and Jon Froggatt to chase. They lived up to the description I'd been given in the clubhouse, looking vulnerable at the back but with the possibility of doing something up front.

Cheetham was the player Mike had advised me to keep and eye on, and he seemed pretty sharp. He nearly got on the end of through balls, and he created a chance for himself too when he turned his marker but was unable to get a shot in.

The Bucks gradually settled down and managed to sustain some pressure. A right wing cross looked as if it was going out for a goal kick but Kevin Curry somehow managed to keep it in and won a corner. From this only a late deflection prevented Froggatt getting clean strike on the edge of the six-yard box. Confidence was found as centre back Hutchinson hit a 40-yard shot. If he was a Brazilian or Paul Gacoigne twelve years ago then this could have been understandable, but a centre back? To be fair though it was only a foot over. Wood was even closer; his 30-yard lob was wonderfully weighted and would have dropped in if had it not been for the goalie's hand tipping over.

Just after the half-hour they won another corner. It swung in and Railway's Phil Walker tried to control it but it shot into the net past a statuesque goalkeeper. "Perhaps that will quieten their fans", a man near me suggested. He was wrong as an even louder chorus of "Super, super rail", rang out. They even had a chance for an instant reply when striker Sunley had a chance laid on for him on the edge of the penalty box but he put it wide. The half ended 1-0.

Harrogate Railway had hit the headlines earlier on in the year when they got to the second round of the FA Cup, the furthest any NCE club have ever got. They eventually lost 3-1 at home to Bristol City. As I have said before the FA Cup brings glamour to many non-league clubs and Buxton fans may have been imagining themselves in that place. However the blessing nearly turned to curse as the club almost fell apart over an argument over money. Railway players demanded £1,000 each for the second round tie, whilst the club offered £200 per man. The manager and team then walked out for a week, during which time the reserves stepped in and in the Rocky or Up'n'Under tradition won their games against the odds. Public opinion quickly turned when they found out that the players had already shared £20,000, and the rebels soon returned to the fold.

The FA Cup for Buxton had been pretty barren, having never got to the first round proper since 1962. However twelve years earlier they had their best season when they got to the third round before being beaten 4-3 by Aldershot at Silverlands.

The second half had barely got started when Harrogate got themselves back in the game. A Buxton defender did well to block a cross, but the ball went straight to Railway skipper Steve Daley who couldn't miss from six yards out.

Buxton fortunately recovered and recaptured their first half form. Mark Calvin, on as a substitute, caught the eye in midfield as he tore around the pitch. Most of Buxton's danger though came from Curry. He'd had a couple of good runs in the first half when he beat a number of players, but hadn't been given enough of the ball. Now he seemed the pivotal player, forcing corners and creating chances. One run saw him play a one-two with Froggatt but his shot was blocked. Later on he took the ball from defence up the field, but was fouled. He picked himself up and ran up and Willis played a quick free kick to him that completely caught out the protesting Railway players.

On 66 minutes goalkeeper Jon Scargill (nicknamed Arthur of course) belted the ball downfield, the ball bounced once and over the bemused Harrogate defence. Cheetham wasn't caught out though and raced through to lob the ball over the goalie to restore the Bucks' lead. For all the criticism of route one, when it works it looks great, well, if it's for your team anyway.

Curry nearly sewed the game up for Buxton minutes later when Holmes laid the ball to him just inside the area, but the shot just missed the top right corner of the net. That was the end of the game for him as manager Ronnie Wright brought him off.

96

People around me were getting nervous. "We've got another 20 minutes to hang on for", a club official muttered. Buxton though seemed to be hanging on in there, with Pinder making a triple tackle, including once on the floor with his body, and the ball was cleared off the line on another occasion. Arthur was catching everything that came near him. At the other end they had chances to make it a more comfortable last few minutes but they strayed offside at crucial moments. When Froggatt managed to get past the defence without the linesman flagging his shot was pushed round for a corner.

The win kept Buxton in fourth spot. Before I left I had a quick chat with Mike again. Promotion was almost impossible this season but they were looking ahead for next year for a concerted effort to go back to the Northern Premier League. "The club is doing OK but we need to be back where we belong", he said, "we used to be two levels higher until a few years ago. We get almost 300 for our games which is far better than most other teams in the league". Buxton supporters certainly feel they should be higher up. On their website supporters referred to the NCE League as a 'glorified pub league'.

He was able to satisfy my curiosity on one point. Buxton has been linked with the Dukes of Devonshire for hundreds of years, with the family owning great chunks of the town. The Crescent was built by one of the Dukes, well not personally obviously. Silverlands itself was bought from the Chatsworth estate and the current Duke is club patron. After coming across his name at Chesterfield and Matlock I asked Mike what contact they had with him. As I suspected, his Grace was not a regular on the terraces. "We did invite him to our 125th anniversary dinner last month. He sent a nice letter declining it though. It seems he doesn't go out much at night nowadays". Oh well, bang goes another mental image.

Buxton 2 – 1 Harrogate Railway
Walker (o.g.) 29   Davey 48
Cheetham 66

Buxton: Scargill, P Wood, Mason, Anson (Calvin 45), Hutchinson, Willis, Holmes, Pinder, Froggatt, Cheetham, Curry (Fretwell 73). Sub (not used) Francis

Harrogate: Neale, Gray (Anderson 65), McLean, Wilson (Wrigley), Danby, Walker, Ames, Davey, Sunley, Smith, Gore

Attendance 272

Glapwell v Thackley
Hall Corner
Northern Counties East League Premier Division
Saturday 29th March 2003

I should have been at Pride Park to see Derby play Millwall, but during the week the match was called off due to international call-ups. This amused Rams fans no end because of the three players called up two were not even likely to be selected for Derby. However it did give me a chance to come and see Glapwell.

Glapwell is a small village in North East Derbyshire, in between Chesterfield, Bolsover and Shirebrook. Like many villages in that part of the county it had been a colliery community. I saw two memorials in the village to the colliery, which had been open from 1882-1973. Both featured small models of the winding wheels. I wonder what memorials they will erect to modern industries in the future? Call centres, insurance companies and computer chip plants do not integrate themselves as part of an area as coal mining did.

More well known is Hardwick Hall, which is just a couple of miles away and has made the last twelve of a national survey of the best Country Houses in Britain. Thomas Hobbes had tutored at the Hall and is buried at the local church. In his political work, Leviathan, he said, "The life of man, solitary, poor, nasty, brutish, and short". Being tutored by him must have been a joyous experience! However I am sure many depressed football fans could sympathise with him.

I only came across the club when I saw a link on a website. "Don't let the size of this village put you off, they have a great football team". It is indeed a small village, but they have gone up so far and so fast that the local doctor must be worn out treating nosebleeds. Formed in 1985 from the remnants of a pub team, Young Vanish FC, they rose from the Sutton & Skegby League to the NCE Premier Division in just twelve years, winning a cabinet full of silverware on route. In 1998 they beat Belper Town, Ilkeston Town and Matlock Town to win the Derbyshire Senior Cup. Now in their third season in the premier division they looked pretty secure being mid table each season.

Inside the ground I took up a place near the half way line by their stand. According to the programme it could seat 100, although that looked over generous. A three generation family stood nearby. "Did Chris Waddle ever play a proper game for you?" I asked, revealing one of the few bits of information I knew about Glapwell.

"Don't think so", the Grandfather replied, "he just played a friendly in August and hasn't been seen here since." Glapwell had proudly announced his signing at the start of the season, with the former England international's pen pic on the website along with the other players. The crucial sentence though is the one that says, "Except when otherwise tied by media commitments". Considering I keep hearing him on Radio 5 on a Saturday afternoon I wasn't surprised that I never saw his name when I checked Glapwell's reports. Incidentally neighbours South Normanton of the Central Midlands League had announced Waddle had signed for them just this week. He has turned up for the obligatory photo opportunities but I don't think it would be worth a speculative visit there to see him play.

"We seem to win two games and lose one", the Grandfather told me when I asked how they had been doing this season. The disease of inconsistency that afflicts 80% of clubs is here too. How many times do managers say they need to sort out their club's consistency?

Thackley, who gave the footballing world Ian Ormandroyd (Bradford City, Aston Villa and of course Derby

County), began the stronger. Glapwell, unfortunately for me playing in black and white stripes, were on the back foot but competing well. Both sides were fairly strong and had a bit of nouse, and the referee was kept on his toes to spot when the teams overstepped the mark.

Up front Glapwell kept up the tradition of striking duos with Yates and Bates. Whether Radio's Derby or Sheffield had approached them yet for a Saturday morning programme I can't say. Yates looked the stronger, putting himself about, whilst his partner looked to nip in for any chance. Precious few chances were created though against a strong Thackley defence. Yates had a couple of half chances, hitting one just wide from a tight angle, and then hitting another well over. If Yates and Bates don't work out then they even have Ashton and Ashley in midfield.

On 17 minutes Thackley scored when Andy Patterson wasn't picked up on the right hand side of the penalty area and he hit a strong shot past Glapwell's deputy goalkeeper Herring. Glapwell tried to respond but the best chance was a shot by Yates from a tight angle from a ball over the top. The only other chances they could muster were a couple of long range shots from ex-pro Neil Ashley.

Towards the end of the half a ball down the Glapwell right wing was chased by Ashton and Thackley's Riley, but the linesman flagged for a foul by the home player when he clipped his opponent's heels and brought him down. Ashton was not amused, telling the linesman, "His legs are six foot long".

"Doesn't mean you can stand on them", came back the reply.

An interesting debate on the laws of football could have ensued when one supporter shouted to the linesman that it couldn't have been a foul because it was unintentional. That's a new one on me.

At half time I wondered about trying to find the club shop that was mentioned in the programme in order to buy a pen. A sunny afternoon meant that I hadn't bothered taking my coat out of the car, and my pen was in the coat. The lack of detail in my report is resulting from trying to remember everything that happens. However, when I asked my neighbours where the shop was they were taken aback. "Club shop?" the Dad said, "I've never seen anything like that in all the time I've been coming."

We got chatting about football, as football fans generally do. The Grandfather usually went to see Sheffield United, who had reached two cup semi-finals and were third in Division One. Although I am following Derbyshire football, administrative boundaries are often ignored when it comes to where places lean towards, just as I've mentioned the Burton links with Derby. Glapwell for instance has strong links to South Yorkshire and Nottinghamshire. I asked them who their local rivals were. "Worksop and Eastwood I suppose", the Dad answered immediately. Both of these are over the border. "There's a big rivalry with Eastwood at the moment", the dad explained, "partly because a lot of players go back and forth between the two."

The teams came back out, and as is the custom nowadays we had a new linesman in front of us. The Dad decided it was time for a bit of psychological warfare to aid Glapwell. "My wife loves it when a lino stands near us. It means she can give him stick for 45 minutes". Incidentally the wife was looking just as calm as she had done in the first half.

The linesman was not perturbed. "That's OK 'cause I get it 24 hours a day at home". A good retort is probably a mandatory part of their training.

Apart from a Glapwell substitute, former Eastwood player Davies, the second half was like the first, with a strong contest being shaded by Thackley. It could have been different if Richard Smith's early free kick hadn't gone agonisingly past the right hand post.

The Grandfather had pointed out that the Thackley custodian resembled David James. Well Glapwell must have wished that Mr James was here instead because every cross and ball into the box was collected comfortably by Aaron Brian. It would take something special to score past him, and that had never looked likely all match.

Glapwell defended well but the Yorkshiremen still created a number of chances that went begging. Herring saved the day on one occasion when he came out to the edge of the area to block a shot with his legs. It was no surprise though when they scored another. A ball from the left wing found centre forward Patterson unmarked. Whilst one defender appealed for offside despite being the one who played him onside, the striker took his time and blasted it in from a tight angle.

The home side never really looked like equalising. As the Son summed up, "There's no-one holding the ball up, it just keeps coming back". That was the difference between the teams. Eventually there was a good cross that didn't go to Brian. Unfortunately the two Glapwell players in the box also missed it. At least they were safe from relegation though.

Glapwell 0 – 2 Thackley
Patterson 17, 84

Glapwell: Herring, Colliver, Magee, Simmonite, Hogg, Smith, Ashley, Varley (Walker 45), Yates, Bates (Dooley 62), Ashton (Davies 69)

Thackley: Brian, Nelson, Lawler, Riley, Sugden, Fletcher (Hillam 65), Senior, Oliver, Patterson, Morris (Carberry 77), Brooks

Attendance: 70

103

April Musings

April was here, the clocks had gone forward, and the end of the season was within sight. Up and down the country fans, manager, players and the media were working out league tables and permutations on a daily basis. Six points clear/behind (delete as appropriate) and six games left, or whatever your club's position happened to be.

In the Unibond First Division Alfreton were stumbling towards the championship. After their run of 26 games without defeat was ended by local rivals Belper Town, they had gone six matches without a win. Crucial injuries to the strikers Godber and Goddard may have been an important factor. Even after a home defeat to Chorley they were still seven points clear of the play-offs and favourites for promotion.

Belper and Matlock were both battling for fifth place and the final play-off place. A further hurdle would be ground grading and whilst Belper had already achieved this the Gladiators were still awaiting their verdict. Needless to say the three sets of fans were filling each other's message boards with good luck messages and congratulating each other on each other's ground improvements. OK, so I'm kidding. To view some people's postings you would have thought that the decisions made Watergate look irrelevant.

The other big Derbyshire promotion battle was in the NCE First Division, with Mickleover, Long Eaton and Shirebrook in the top three places. Mickleover, having signed former Ram Jason Kavanagh from Burton, looked favourites to win the title since they were top with matches in hand. They were having an outstanding season having also just got to the Derbyshire Senior Cup Final and the Wilkinson Sword Trophy. They were also a whisker away from reaching the President's Cup Final too. Which other side would join them was anyone's guess.

Coming down in their place would be Borrowash Victoria, unless a miracle took place. Bottom of the Premier Division for most of the season, the Vics had won three of their last seven matches but it looked to be too late to save them from relegation.

In the Central Midlands League Graham Street Prims were second from bottom and struggling to pick up points. Heanor Town had slipped down to mid table.

Chesterfield's form had also dipped since I'd visited. They were now seven points above relegation with seven matches to play, or something similar. Manager Dave Rushbury never had all the fans behind him when they were 7th, so you can imagine how popular he was now. Perhaps the signing of two players from Middlesbrough in the past fortnight would help.

Burton Albion had dropped down the table too, but recent wins had propelled them up into the top half of the table and within a couple of weeks talk of relegation was replaced by dreams of the play-offs. Who said football fans are fickle?

Down in South Derbyshire Gresley fluctuated between seventh and eighth place as their season plodded along. One item of note was a presentation to Richard Wardle who had become the longest serving player in the club's history.

Ilkeston Town v Worcester City
New Manor Ground
Southern (Dr Martens) Premier Division
Saturday 12th April 2003

I had intended visiting Ilkeston, or Ilson as the locals call it, earlier on in the season when they played Chelmsford City, but a downpour had left the pitch looking like a practice area for Ellen MacArthur and the match was called off. Perhaps the delay was good because I was now seeing an Ilkeston side that was looking to extend a seven match unbeaten run. Unfortunately they would still be relegated unless they won today, not even halfway through April, which gives you an idea of how bad their season had been. For whatever reason their season had never got going and Ilkeston had spent most of the season rooted to the bottom.

I knew a bit about Ilkeston from Duncan Payne, who has written the official club history and is an occasional visitor to our library. Although there has been football in Ilkeston for many years, it was only in 1945 that Ilkeston Town FC was formed. They then gradually went up the leagues to the powerful Southern League.

It is amazing to think of Ilkeston, like Gresley, being in the Southern League. Yes I know that I used to think anywhere below Yorkshire was in the 'Deep South', but really how can Derbyshire be southern? Regional leagues have always been problematic. How do you ensure that leagues contain clubs of similar ability and geographic location? Ilkeston has to visit Dover, Tiverton and Weymouth yet most of the Northern Premier League Clubs are far closer. Burton had switched to the NPL and had saved over 1,000 miles of travelling. Of course each league thinks it is stronger, Gresley fans calling the Unibond the Unimportant League when Ilkeston first began contemplating the switch. Plans were afoot to restructure the leagues but whoever had the job clearly had a lot of head scratching to do.

The New Manor Ground is a new stadium and looks quite impressive at this level. Particularly eye-catching is the clock tower in the corner of the ground, a unique feature in the growing trend of identical stadiums. They had had a struggle with their old ground, owned by the council, for many years. Like Long Eaton and other sides they had to move divisions more than once due to the poor state of the ground. It was then a race against time to find a new site to move to before they went under. The local mayor once said that he thought a DIY store would be better than a football ground, which didn't help matters. I just wonder how many would be prepared to spend hours of unpaid time helping out a Home Improvements store.

As I wandered round the ground I asked whether Duncan was here today. After being pointed in various directions I ended up in the stand next to the clock tower. It looked fairly exclusive, having to have a special gate opened and then closed after me, and many of the people wore club blazers. This was a bit different from most matches I've been to. I quickly sat down before anyone threw me out!

The early pressure came from Ilkeston, although they found it hard to get a shot in. This changed on ten minutes when Freestone chased a long ball forward. The last defender tried to muscle Freestone out of the way and leave it for the goalie to grab it, but the striker managed to get round and with the keeper down ready to grab the ball he took it away and then fired in from a tight angle.

Worcester, fifth in the table, were stung into life and then stormed back. The home defence booted the ball clear once, but got into trouble a minute later. Andy Love received a backpass at the edge of the penalty area with striker Webster bearing down on him. A rushed kick rebounded off Webster and looped over Love and we all held our breath to see if it would drop into the net. It merely hit the crossbar, but Webster was first to the ball and headed in the equaliser.

The Robins in turn stormed back, and O'Connor forced a corner when he cut in from the right wing and his dangerous cross was knocked out by Worcester. It was O'Connor himself who headed the ball in direct from the corner kick and the home crowd went wild. Tannoy announcer Mic Capill, sitting just behind me, went and announced the goal, but the chap sitting next to me, smoking a large cigar, called out that the ref had disallowed it. I looked around but everyone still seemed to be celebrating, and I don't think anyone believed Mr Cigarman until the Worcester goalie took the free kick. Whatever infringement had taken place had eluded almost everyone in the ground.

The nickname Robins, so called because of their red and white kit, endeared them to me because it was also the nickname of my favourite Rugby League team Hull Kingston Rovers. The robin was on the badge, but for a while it became a white ball up a tree. This dated back to an infamous FA Cup-tie at home to Rochdale in 1951 in front of 9,000 fans. They had to use a white ball, unusual in those days, and it got stuck up a tree. It took so long to get it down that it was feared that they might have to abandon the game and the story went down in folklore.

The game surely couldn't keep up the frenetic pace of the last five minutes, and indeed it drifted along for rest of the half. Niggly fouls broke up play, and neither side could create clear cut chances, although they tried their hardest. O'Connor and Freestone both kept running but the Worcester defence stood firm. At the other end it looked similar with City causing problems but Woolley and Lever at centre-back, although not completely dominant, did enough.

Drama was reserved for the last minute, as O'Connor got goalside of a defender but before he could shoot he was pulled back. The referee didn't give a penalty, but perhaps that was OK since O'Connor was so offside that even home fans admitted it.

At half-time a raffle seller came round. "Anyone want a 50:50 ticket?" he called out. I was in two minds whether to buy one, but when no one responded he just went away. Mickleover's Mr Raffleman would have been appalled.

Since I was unsure whether I should have been in this stand, I decided not to go for a drink in case I wasn't let back in. Instead I went to chat to the Ilkeston fans opposite me. After a good performance from Ilkeston I wondered how they were in this position. "We didn't win enough matches", one of them, Mick, said simply. Football is not a complicated game.

"Everything went against us", he elaborated. "All the 50:50 balls and decisions went against us. Take the first goal, that would have been disallowed earlier on." There is little to be said when you face bad luck.

I asked him whether they could come back next year. "Depends who stays and who goes. Most of these players would be too good to play in the Western Division."

"Why are we down here then", Mick's friend piped in. Relegated teams are often full of players who in theory are too good to play in the division below. I had heard elsewhere that Ilkeston, through paying comparatively well for that league, attracted some players who were just looking for a nice pay-day and let their managers down.

Manager Charlie Bishop had obviously fired up the troops again, since they won an early corner which didn't drop kindly for them. O'Connor then dribbled the ball into the area but his lob hit the post.

Another left wing corner was won. A Worcester player was down injured on the goalline. "He's off the pitch", Mick and few others cried out. "Carry on with the match, he's just putting it on". Football fans are never the most sympathetic of people. When it was eventually taken City half cleared it, before O'Connor disposed a defender, then skipped past two players and hit it into the back of the net with the goalie going the wrong way. It was an outstanding goal and had almost everyone in the stand on their feet.

Three minutes later it got even better when Ilkeston won a right wing free kick. Hemmings send over a wonderful cross to the far post, which Freestone headed into the net from six yards out. Three one up and mission impossible was incredibly still on.

Freestone is a former Premiership striker, having played and scored for, yes you guessed it, Middlesbrough. After being given too few opportunities he went to Northampton, Hartlepool and Shrewsbury. A number of non-league players I have seen this season have been former professionals. Most are players who spent one or two seasons at league clubs before dropping down after never establishing themselves. Others are like Freestone, having played a number of seasons professionally before struggling to find another club once they hit their thirties. A small number are very successful professionals who enjoy their football so much that they continue even when most of their contemporaries have packed in. Duncan had been telling me that he first started coming when Kenny Burns played for Ilkeston. Even this season Mark Walters had played a couple of games for the Robins.

Ilkeston fans couldn't relax too much, since a few minutes later City got the ball in the Ilson box. Andy Love looked to have got to the ball first but the striker impeded him and then backed into him before knocking the ball back for Middleton to score. Surely it wouldn't stand, but it did. Straight forward, bog standard goals were not going to be scored today.

Ilkeston shaded the rest of the match, but Worcester looked dangerous on occasion too. There was plenty of hard work, with Freestone and O'Connor running all afternoon long, but there was a fair amount of skill on show too. O'Connor played a beautiful one-two with Murdock to create a wonderful chance. Defender Woolley, having scored in the past two matches, almost made it three in a row as he had one header pushed round for a corner and another was headed off the line

City had couple of late chances. Love managed to get a hand to a close range effort to push it away with minutes remaining to save the day, but a voice near me screamed, "Lovie, you're supposed to catch the ball!" Who'd be a goalkeeper, some people are never satisfied.

The last action of the afternoon though involved O'Connor and Freestone again as once again the former went a run and beat two players before unselfishly squaring it to Freestone for his hat-trick. Freestone blasted the shot, but the goalie got some part of his body to it to slow the ball down, giving a defender time to get back and clear it. The final whistle went and the home fans around me gave a huge cheer. The dressing rooms were just below so they all stood and gave the players a standing ovation. Eight matches unbeaten and they were not relegated yet.

In the programme notes manager Charlie Bishop bemoaned only getting the job in November and claimed they could have been challenging for the Conference instead of being bottom. This didn't entirely convince Robins fans, but he had clearly changed things because although I had been here 13 months ago none of today's 16 players had been playing that day. Already this season an amazing 59 players had been used! Ironically Bishop had been caretaker manager briefly last season. Gresley Rovers manager John McGinley, the former Bolton and Scotland striker got the permanent job instead.

Ilkeston appeared to have a reputation of having big names. Ex-Derby County and Wales player Leighton James was briefly manager, current Lincoln City manager Keith Alexander was another former Robins chief, as were John McGovern and former Chesterfield goalie and Derbyshire wicket-keeper Chris Marples. Big names however do not guarantee success.

Ilkeston Town 3 – 2 Worcester City
Freestone 10, 53   Webster 12, Middleton 60
O'Connor 50

Ilkeston: Love, Hudson, Atkinson, Woolley, Lever, Robinson, Murdock (Westwood 85), Hemmings, O'Connor, Freestone, Coates. Subs not used: Brown, Williams, Anderson, Evans

Worcester: McDonnell , Davies (Owen 54), Jones (Carty 46), Heeley , Shail, Holloway, Middleton, Foy, Webster, H Counsell (Hadley 81), Wilde.

Attendance: 435

On Tuesday fifth from bottom Grantham won. Ilkeston were not down yet though. No, if they won every remaining match by four clear goals and Grantham lost their remaining games by four clear goals then the improbable could still be achieved...

Mickleover Sports v Alfreton Town
Station Road
Derbyshire Senior Cup Final – 1st leg
Tuesday 15th April 2003

It might not have been the FA Cup final at Wembley but there was a bit of atmosphere at Station Road. Certainly there were more cars around than when I had last visited. I was returning to see the first leg of the Derbyshire Senior Cup where Mickleover were in their first final but Alfreton were the current holders. Both sides were having outstanding seasons, with Mickleover having gained promotion on Saturday and Alfreton just a win away from doing the same in their division.

The Derbyshire Senior Cup dates back to 1883/84 when Staveley beat Derby Midland 2-1 at the County Ground, Derby. Over 7,000 fans from all over the county turned up to see this spectacle. The cup is the subject of Duncan Payne's latest research and he'd been popping into the library to look up newspaper reports during the last couple of years.

It is easy to forget how times have changed in those past 115 years. There's a story that Graham Street Prims reached the semi-final in the early years. They were forced to withdraw though because they couldn't get up to Tideswell to play it in time. In those days most players worked in the morning and had to travel to away games by train. However I'm afraid that this may be another myth. In their early years the Chapel Boys rarely got past the early rounds and Duncan hadn't heard the story. However it may have been one of the lesser competitions such as the Derbyshire Medals or Derbyshire Junior Cup.

The Cup was soon split into regions to avoid the above situation, and when it was reunited in 1912 only four clubs could enter, and from 1925-37 it was just for Derby County and Chesterfield. It then became a competition for the leading non-league clubs, which it still is today. It would be easy to dismiss it as a Mickey Mouse competition, and this season the early rounds did see the bigger clubs resting players. However wherever there is local rivalry there is plenty of pride and bragging rights at stake. Over the past 12 years Glapwell, Glossop North End, Borrowash and Stapenhill had all gatecrashed the final at the expense of the 'bigger' sides.

This season Mickleover were making their first appearance after beating Borrowash Victoria 3-0, Ilkeston Town 2-0 and Gresley Rovers 4-0. Alfreton were back to defend their title after seeing off Ripley Town 3-0, Glossop North End 3-0, and Belper Town 1-0.

I'd dashed straight from work so I went and bought a cheeseburger for my tea from a van inside the ground. After going nineteen years with only having one pie and perhaps a couple of chocolate bars from stadium catering outlets I was suddenly getting to be a regular.

The chap stood next to me was from Matlock. "Have you seen Alfreton already?" he asked me after I told him about my quest. "They are a very good side and should win this easily". I explained that I had seen them at the start of the season before they had got into their stride. I was looking forward to see them eight months later, even if the team had been much altered.

"Not a bad crowd", I commented, estimating around 250-300 people here, far more than when I last visited.

"We might have had a thousand or more if a really big team like Belper or Matlock had got through", Mr Matlock said, perhaps a little sadly.

From the start Alfreton looked the stronger side and spent most of the first few minutes in the Mickleover half. An early free kick had to be headed behind and then from the corner Hindley hit the ball just over the bar. This pattern continued with corners and crosses cleared as best they could. The biggest let off for Sports was a shot from Johnson that went over from just six yards out.

"It's pretty one sided", Mr Matlock commented.

"Yeah", I agreed, "Alfreton look so much stronger."

"And more skilful", he added. "You can tell there are a couple of divisions between them". Sports were struggling to get forward, and when Alfreton were in possession they couldn't get hold of it until it came to the last ditch tackle or clearance. The ball was sprayed about the park with supreme confidence. Ryan Hindley in particular stood out and he seemed to move at will through the Mickleover midfield and defence.

The home side did show some signs of encouragement, as they tried to take on Alfreton and they showed bits of skill. Wraith was set free in a promising position on the left but his cross was caught by goalkeeper Turner. The waves of blue shirts kept coming though with some fluent moves that would have tested many better sides than Mickleover. The goal hadn't come though and skipper Steve Heath let Sports off again when he headed over from just three yards.

On the half-hour the blue shirted Alfreton opened Mickleover's defence again. A ball was lobbed into the penalty box, which Steve Johnson flicked with his foot onto the crossbar. Hindley was steaming into the area and blasted the ball into the net to open the scoring and send the visiting fans wild. It was surprising that Hindley, who had been in an FA Youth Cup Final with Sheffield Wednesday, was not a regular in the Alfreton line-up.

"Have you got your tickets", boomed out a voice to my right. Yes, it was Mr Raffleman. Anyone who caught his eye or paused was pounced upon. I steeled myself to look straight ahead at the action, where both sides exchanged half chances before going in for the break.

In the second half Mickleover tried to get back into the match. The front players were comparatively small but battled hard with Hobson and Heath. They were not afraid to play some adventurous football but whilst in the first half this had broken down too soon, they now managed to get into the penalty box. Parkin won one header to set up Karl Payne whose volley was tipped over by Turner. Cunningham put a chance wide and a corner soon afterwards saw Hobson get his head in the way to stop a Mickleover player getting in clear header on goal from a corner.

Sports were left ruing those missed chances as Alfreton stormed down the other end. Goddard set up Hindley to score his second. Left back Corin Holness, who looked be one of Mickleover's more talented players, forced another great save from Turner. The holders put the game beyond doubt by scoring a third soon after. John Knapper, who'd almost rejoined Ilkeston as coach in the autumn, sent in a good cross, which Dolby directed past the advancing goalkeeper.

It is hard to believe some of the negative comments on the Alfreton website. Almost every other message slates various players and calls for manager David Lloyd to resign. Yes, Alfreton in their first season back in the Unibond League are a few points clear and some fans think Lloyd is the worst manager in the league. Just what do they want? Turner is one of the players criticised, yet today he must surely have won them over with some outstanding saves. However some fans have their suspicions that the posters are really Belper or Matlock fans.

The match was still open with chances for both sides. Holness tried a bicycle kick that appeared to have been handled by an Alfreton defender, whilst at the other end Knapper had a header well saved. We even saw Mays try another of his backheels that he had demonstrated against Worsbrough. The confidence each had developed throughout their season had been carried into the match.

I was torn between which team to support, which is unusual for me because I am normally very decisive about who I want to win. Alfreton fans had chanted "No one likes us, we don't care", and I did consider going over and saying that I actually quite like them, but decided that this was probably not what they wanted to hear. I had feelings for Mickleover too, and I certainly wanted them to get at least one goal back to gain some credibility. More than once they gained possession in the area but a determined Alfreton defence got bodies in the way and prevented a shot coming in. Even when Turner finally made a mistake and missed a high cross the ball bounced over the bar.

As the game faded Alfreton took control and camped in the Sports half. Substitute Robshaw crossed for Dolby to get his second. Mr Matlock and many others decided to call it a night. In injury time though Wilson couldn't hold a shot and Robshaw tapped in the ball to get on the scoresheet.

Alfreton were 5-0 winners but it was cruel because Mickleover didn't deserve to lose by that scoreline. That's football though, and Alfreton now could concentrate on winning the league before the second leg at North Street. Just what the team would be I don't know. The Alfreton moaners would no doubt still be dissatisfied, bemoaning at not winning 10-0, and criticising Turner for not scoring a hat-trick, but when are fans ever satisfied?

Mickleover Sports 0 – 5 Alfreton Town
Hindley 35, 54
Dolby 59, 86
Robshaw 90

Mickleover: Wilson, Broadhurst (Warren 80), Holness (Stevens 73), Wood, Reynolds, Yeoman (Smith 77), Mays, Wraith, Parkin, Cunningham, Payne

Alfreton: Turner, Circuit, Highfield, Hobson, Heath, Knapper, Hindley (Tyler 82), Johnson, Askey, Goddard (Robshaw 75), Dolby. Sub (not used) Bettney

Attendance: 285

Derby County v Millwall
Pride Park
Nationwide Football League Division 1
Wednesday 16th April 2003

I know I have already mentioned about Derby's season so far on a few occasions, but I thought I would give you a quick resume of their busy season.

Some of Derby's most experienced and best players are paid to leave the club. Whilst this is being negotiated they are not even played, earning their vast salaries for doing nothing. Poom is sold for less than half what Everton offered during the summer. Derby players are not paid for weeks as the banks refuse to extend the overdraft beyond £30 million.

Brian Richardson, who had guided Coventry City to a £50 million debt, is asked to help sell players at Derby and raise money. He doesn't sell a single player and fails to raise any money via a bond. He tells the press that Derby would let Gregory leave to become manager of Sunderland and implies he is a director, before Lionel Pickering finally bows to the fans demands and ditches him.

Chief Executive Keith Loring is linked with the vacant post of Chief Executive to the FA, but he says that he is happy at Derby and going nowhere. A week later he suddenly resigns and is not replaced. Players are asked to defer part of their salaries until the summer. Derby cannot afford to pay Sheffield United the last instalment of Lee Morris's transfer fee.

International strikers Strupar and Ravanelli are both out long term with injuries. Deon Burton is recalled from a loan spell at Portsmouth and then after scoring some goals is sold off for just £250,000.

Whilst the team is struggling Gregory chooses to play a 16 year old and a 15 year old school boy as a woeful Derby are knocked out of the FA Cup by lowly Brentford. Christie and Riggott are loaned out on the promise of £2.5million in the summer instead of the higher sums offered for them last year. Craig Burley turns down a loan move to stay at Derby. Despite playing really well in a reserve match and the first team struggling he is left out against Stoke. He then goes on the radio to criticise Gregory, and tell everyone that he still has not been paid since September and his car park pass has been revoked. Burley's physio then sues Gregory for medical negligence.

Forest beat Derby in a local derby to leave the Rams staring at a relegation battle. Gregory is suspended by the Rams, for reasons not even the usually over imaginative rumour mill could fathom. Mark Lillis is appointed caretaker manager, and decides to leave out Ravanelli and Burley from the squad for the defeat at Sheffield Utd. Lillis then goes off to help coach Northern Ireland and in his absence Craig's uncle is appointed interim manager instead and Billy McEwan returns as coach after winning his unfair dismissal case. Assistant Manager Ross MacClaren and the physio are also suspended. Valakari, Burley, Oakes, Kinkladze and Ravanelli are recalled, some of them from a wilderness beyond the cold, and play really well as they help Derby win for the first time since early February.

Rampage Radio is axed because it is losing money. Former player Rod Thomas, sacked as Chief Scout by Gregory, is appointed Director of Football by the chairman, despite a limited football management CV and an already bulging Rams backroom staff. Keith Pearson, disgusted by this act after having to make many loyal employees redundant, announces his resignation.

Er, I think that's it, but it has been hard to keep track. The usual response from Rams fans has been to say that things can't get any worse, and that they are past worrying.

Ian Hall, Radio Derby's expert summariser, said that the only surprise left was that Brian Clough was to be the next goalkeeper.

With the club's huge debt I felt a little guilty that I was getting in for free. I'd won two tickets via Radio Derby a few weeks earlier before the game was postponed. It had taken a few goes at winning the tickets, but by that particular week I was back in the habit. As a child I used to enter every competition going on Radio Cleveland. Perhaps it was due to my keen competitive instinct that I would dash to the phone like a gambler to a bookies on Grand National day as I won theme park tickets, book tokens, trainers and a tea bag. Yes, I won a tea bag (unused) but who cares because I had won.

Today I am not so driven. I am more relaxed and when I knew the answer to a competition on Christmas Eve I decided that an extra five minutes in a warm bed was more compelling. Once I'd got up though and heard that no one had got the answer I cracked and phoned in to win a Radio Derby mug to go with my Radio Cleveland breakfast bowl.

At least there was now a larger air of optimism from Derby fans. Dorothy was fairly positive about their chances, and Mr Thompson was the most optimistic I'd seen for a long time. It is incredible what a difference a couple of wins make. It could also have been due to weather. It was the hottest April day since 1949 and the heat was almost stifling as we made our way to Pride Park. David, a friend since Sixth Form College was coming with me. He's another Boro fan, and has been a season ticket holder for the past ten seasons even when living in Nottingham, Basingstoke and Derby.

We had barely had chance to get our seats and get settled in before Millwall scored. Under the challenge of visiting striker McCammon, Andy Oakes spilled the ball and Neil Harris blasted in the loose ball via Tommy Mooney's head.

Derby under George Burley seem to be made of stronger stuff than before and they attacked back with purpose. When Derby appeared to have kicked the ball out Murray chased and kept it in. He then pulled the ball back for the enigmatic Kinkladze to hit a beautiful shot from the corner of the penalty box across the goal and in for a wonderful equaliser.

A player that both David and I were interested in seeing was Fabrizio Ravanelli, a player whose reputation precedes him and is often greater than his actual contributions. David thought he was off the pace a bit, but I was more impressed than I thought I'd be, or perhaps even wanted to be. He still plainly had class, and he also had a hunger that drove him to chase back passes, close down defenders and chase lost causes. As ever he seemed so good with the ball at his feet and his back to goal. From one of these situations he turned his man and fired a shot that hit the inside of the post and bounced just out. On another occasion he was through on goal but could only hit the ball straight at the goalie.

Whilst Derby looked quite good going forward they were vulnerable at the back. Millwall's tactics were not subtle as they hit balls over the top or else took it down the wing and crossed. However time and again Harris and McCammon found themselves in space and the five man defence struggled to cope. Ironically it was on loan striker Tommy Mooney, playing as emergency centre back, who looked the most effective of the three centre backs. The trouble was that Derby too often were their own worst enemy as they played suicidal passes.

The half finished all square. It had been pretty entertaining although some the excitement had come from mistakes. One person I hoped was enjoying it was Inge. I had met him that morning in the library whilst he was reading old Derby County reports in the Derby Evening Telegraph. He's a teacher back in Norway, but has been coming over to the Rams every Easter holiday for the past

20 years. Thinking about it he must have seen a wide variety of ups and downs in that period. I asked him why he had chosen Derby. "Back in 1970", he explained, "they started showing English matches on Norwegian TV. I saw Archie Gemmill, the muddy Baseball Ground pitch and I fell in love with Derby County." He paused as he recalled those halcyon days, "and of course Brian Clough."

Today Inge was part of Pride Park's lowest ever league crowd, 21,014. Perhaps the public were fed up of a dreadful season, or perhaps they were attracted by the virtual title decider on Sky of Arsenal v Manchester United. Those who had ventured out were making their feelings clear as choruses of, "Stand up if you want Burley", and "One George Burley" regularly echoed round the ground.

For the second half Lee Grant replaced Oakes in goal. A shoulder injury sustained from a heavy collision with McCammon had obviously been more serious than first thought. Neither goalkeeper was tested much early on though as the teams struggled to create openings. It took quarter of an hour before the Rams had their first opportunity as a good passing move released Ravanelli down the right. Unfortunately only Kinkladze was in the box for Derby and the pass wasn't quite pinpoint enough.

Derby's defensive frailties were cruelly exposed minutes later as a Ritchie back pass was too short and McCammon headed the ball past the advancing Grant and he remained composed enough to control the ball and knock it into the net.

Derby vainly tried to find the equaliser. At times they had plenty of possession, but actually shooting was a different matter. When they did Craig Burley hit his shot wide, and Valakari put his just over. It looked as if it was not to be their day when Craig Burley hit the post and a Kinkladze free kick was pushed round for a corner. As time ran out Boertien and Ravanelli both hit shots well wide.

123

Until the game with Norwich ten days ago Derby were staring relegation in the face, but although they lost today they certainly didn't look that bad. Walking out of the ground David and I discussed the match. "If Derby had had a couple of good defenders and a goalie they would have won it", David thought, "and could be challenging for promotion."

"Such as Riggott, Higginbotham and Poom?" I suggested. The Rams had looked OK, and certain players showed touches of class. Even some of the younger players such as Boertien showed skill in glimpses. But whereas Derby worked hard for their openings, Millwall seemed to find gaps at the back more easily and punished Derby for their mistakes.

So what would the future hold for the Rams? No one had a clue, beyond the fact that Derby would still be in Division one. At least the past couple of weeks had given the fans a bit more confidence.

Derby County 1 – 2 Millwall
Kinkladze 9   Harris 5,
                         McCammon 63

Derby: Oakes (Grant 45); Jackson, Barton (Mills 49), Ritchie, Mooney, Boertien; Burley, Valakari; Kinkladze; Ravanelli, Bolder. Subs (not used) McLeod, Murray, Lee

Millwall: Warner, Lawrence, Nethercott, Ward, Ryan, Ifill, Wise, Roberts, Livermore, Harris (Ashikodi 90), McCammon (Claridge 89)

Attendance: 21,014

124

Glossop North End v Mossley
Surrey Street
North West Counties League Division One
Monday 21st April 2003

I'd been eagerly looking forward to visiting Glossop, perched up in the North West of the county on the border of Lancashire, all season. Why was this? As David and I entered the town there was nothing out of the ordinary, even if the last part of our journey had been very pleasant as we came over the Pennines near Snakes Pass. The actual ground itself had seen better days and I'm sorry to say wasn't one of the more impressive I'd seen. Their performances hadn't been too good either with them just perched above the relegation zone, and their league was the equivalent of Buxton, Borrowash and Glapwell's Northern Counties East League.

The reason for my intrigue was that once upon a time this small Derbyshire town boasted a Football League club. If that wasn't enough, for one season they were more successful than Arsenal and Manchester United, spending 1899/1900 in the top flight, whilst the two clubs currently battling for the championship were in the division below. Admittedly that season Glossop only won four games, over Aston Villa, Blackburn, Burnley and Nottingham Forest, but it makes you wonder what could have been. Having seen Arsenal with their international stars at the Riverside two days earlier the idea seems incredible.

The reason that Glossop was the smallest town ever to have a top division team was that they had their own nineteenth century Jack Walker, Sir Samuel Hill-Wood. The area's abundance of fast flowing rivers and streams led to numerous textile mills being established. Money was there to be made and various families succeeded in making their fortunes. These local families were keen to use some of this money for the benefit of the community in worthy projects that the Victorians specialised in. The Dukes of Norfolk, who despite their title lived locally, paid for the town hall, market hall and railway station. The Woods had built a school, swimming pool and hospital.

In the 1860's the mills virtually stopped as the American Civil War prevented raw cotton coming into Britain. With most of the townsfolk unemployed the local bigwigs organised and funded soup kitchens and relief, saying that it would be an embarrassment if they had to go and ask the national Government to help. If you are rolling in money I suppose it is a little easier to help like this, although the sentiment is rather unusual in the 21st century.

It was in this climate that Sam not only gave the football club their ground, but also enabled them to go professional by paying the players wages. He bankrolled them as they got promotion in 1899 and reached the FA Cup quarter-finals in 1909, although the locals gave good support too and up to 8,000 came to see them. They spent most of the Edwardian years in the lower reaches of Division two, but they still proudly clung onto their professional status.

This couldn't last though and after World War One they were unable to resume in the Football League. The cotton industry in Britain was collapsing and the families, including the Duke of Norfolk, were quickly leaving Glossop. Sam left too, and became chairman of Arsenal, a role still held today by a Hill-Wood. The population dropped by a third as the town dropped from 30,000 to 20,000 between 1921 and 1931. Economic reality meant that Glossop now had to play in the Manchester League for the next 37 years. Ironically they now began to win titles and cups but dreams of returning to professional football had gone.

Forecasts of terrible bank holiday weather had not come to pass and we were privileged to have a sunny afternoon for the football. Glancing at the programme David wondered if Mossley's Neil Pointen could be the former

Everton and Man City player. However discussions as to how old he would be if he was still playing were cut short by the unusual sight of both teams making a human tunnel from the dressing rooms. It seems they were honouring the Glossop physio Micky Parr, another unsung non-league hero apparently, who was retiring after many years' service.

The opening quarter of an hour was one way traffic. Glossop, playing in an all blue kit with red trim conceded a free kick just outside the penalty box, and this was beautifully hit home by Mossley's Tony Carroll. Fellow striker Rob Matthews could have added a second but he hit the ball straight at goalkeeper Stuart Williams. He made up for this a few minutes later though with a volley into the back of the net after a long range header had rebounded off the cross bar.

"There's only going to be one winner here", David said after Mossley blasted a shot just over. I reluctantly had to agree with him. After spending a season visiting their website each week I had grown quite fond of North End. At least we had virtually established that the visiting left back was indeed the former professional. Now without his bushy hair and big moustache he had a bit more skill than many others on the pitch although he was not so mobile now.

The Hillmen, Glossop's nickname, finally began to do something. A couple of half chances were created, but these sandwiched a good Mossley effort which hit the crossbar and the rebound went to the goalie. However Glossop got a slice of luck when Mossley's goalkeeper failed to collect a left wing cross and Radcliffe scored from just a couple of feet out. It was to be his last contribution as for whatever reason he was substituted.

"Stop hiding", manager Chris Nicholson screamed out to his players, and this may have had an effect because they suddenly seemed to be right back in the game. Midfielders Steve Jordan and Morris put themselves about and seemed to take charge of the game. Up front Elliott

Prest looked good and nearly equalised whilst left winger Wild showed glimpses of skill here and there.

On 34 minutes the experienced Pointen made a mistake when he tried to control a Glossop long ball instead of just booting it. Prest nipped in and played the ball out wide to Wild who dribbled into the box. His shot was fumbled by the hapless goalie and Morris tapped in the equaliser. Mossley's manager Ally Pickering, stood just a few feet from me and David, was going mad as he berated Pointen and the other players.

At half time we went round to the club-house to see the scores on TV. If any Glossop official happens to be reading this they'll be pleased to know that Dave was very impressed with the prices at the bar.

The Glossop website has an active message board. It had been a difficult season and manager Nicholson had been criticised by various anonymous people, some who claimed to be players. To his credit Nicholson came on and defended himself, and even said he was available to talk to after any match. What an idea if other managers took this approach. Can you imagine Alex Ferguson inviting Man United fans to question his football management over a pint? Or Derby fans being allowed to queue up to quiz John Gregory after another defeat?

Mossley however were in a two horse race to win the title and promotion to the Unibond League. In a reply to my post to the Glossop website I was told that I could spot visiting fans by their two heads and three arms! Yes, Mossley and Glossop were bitter local rivals with all that this entails.

The second half began like the first, with Mosley going up a gear and sustaining pressure. The Hillmen hung on and managed to clear most attacks, and when they couldn't the crossbar came to their rescue. I'd been told to watch out for recent signing Williams, and he looked solid enough in goal.

128

Mossley failed to score during their pressure, and they gradually faded whilst Glossop began to dominate. As the half went on it was the home side that looked most likely to win. It was an amazing turn around and one I'd rarely seen so dramatically in 20 years of watching football. Prest in particular was standing out. He could hold off defenders, move well with the ball, and created chances. Unfortunately putting them away was a little more tricky, and when they finally did the linesman's flag was raised. They also had a good shout for a penalty which was turned down.

With fifteen minutes left many players were struggling. "The difference between these players and the Premier League is that they are not 90 minute players", David observed. To be fair many will have played two days ago after a long season, but it still meant that the game was slowing down. We even saw the rare event of a foul throw given by a referee as Glossop tired.

As the game drew to a close each side tried to raise themselves to claim all the points. Prest won the ball in midfield and attacked but was unable to score and Wild twice flopped down in the Mossley penalty area. Was he going for the penalty? I didn't think so since it would have been more blatant than Jurgen Klinsmann since there was no defender close, but David was less generous in his opinion. Mossley then nearly won it with their first attack for a long time but hit it high and wide.

A point against the top of the table side was an achievement for Glossop, and I was thrilled at the way they came back after their start. It was also a step towards safety.

It is a pleasant drive home through the Peak District, although it does take you through the village voted the ugliest by Radio 5 listeners, Dove Holes. Perhaps that is a little harsh.

The drive home reminded me just how big Derbyshire is. A couple of weeks after moving to Derby I went see one of my sisters in Burnley. After more than and hour and a half I hadn't even reached Glossop. Admittedly I had been going behind a farm vehicle for much of this time but it still brought home the size. Today I didn't see a tractor on the road but it still took over ninety minutes to get back. If it is a bank holiday then it may be worth avoiding driving through Matlock Bath, something that I had unfortunately forgotten.

Glossop North End 2 – 2 Mossley

Radcliffe 26,	Carroll 5
Morris 34	Matthews 15

Glossop: Williams, Niblow, Dodd, Copson, Conlan, Jordan, Morris, Bovis, Radcliffe (Dean 27 (Costello 74)), Prest, Wild

Mossley: Lythe, Jackson (Walton 21), Pointen, Phillips, Taylor (Sheil 37), Coyne, Heaton, Callaghan, Carroll, Matthews, Headley. Sub not used: Pickering

Att: 271

Alfreton Town v Mickleover Sports
North Street
Derbyshire Senior Cup Final – 2nd Leg
Tuesday 29th April 2003

I sometimes wonder how teams manage to keep going when they are in the middle of a losing run or getting thrashed and there is nothing they can do. I imagine it is easy to play when you do well or even just OK, but it must be difficult to carry on and believe that you can change things when everything is against you.

In 1981 my Dad took me to watch a Rugby League match between Hull Kingston Rovers and Bradford. Hull KR were so comprehensively outclassing Bradford that when the Bradford skipper was sent off he signalled for his team mates to come off the pitch with him and they conceded the match. My only memory of the match is the Rovers players stood in the middle of the pitch for ten minutes not knowing what to do before the match was declared over. I was recently intrigued to find out more about that match and discovered that Bradford actually claimed that they went off because they felt the referee was biased, but if that was a valid reason no sports team would ever take the field.

OK, so today's match wasn't on such a dramatic scale, but there was no doubt as to who would win the cup. In the club shop a couple of Alfreton fans were discussing the game and one asked if extra time would be played if the scores were level.

"Extra time!" his friend cried out loudly. "If we have extra time tonight there'll be a riot and the club house will be burnt to the ground".

Most people though were not expecting enough fans to make a riot even if Mickleover defied the odds. On the

Alfreton website a number of fans admitted they would give the game a miss since it was a foregone conclusion. This seems such a shame considering that it was a cup final. Perhaps there wasn't as much prestige as I'd thought. Many people seemed to think that it should go back to a one game match at a neutral venue, perhaps Pride Park or the Recreation Ground. Even Causeway Lane and the New Manor Ground were suggested. The final used to be played at the Baseball Ground until 1966, and in 1956 12,000 had watched Ilkeston beat Heanor in the final there. The problem was that after Derby County had taken their cut and the Derbyshire FA had their slice then the finalist could be left with not enough to even cover their travelling costs so would make a loss on their great achievement. Mark, who runs the shop, optimistically thought that today there might be 300 if the rain stopped.

I got chatting to Mark about Alfreton's prospects for the future now the First Division title had been assured and promotion to Premier Division was confirmed. "We should do OK", he said confidently. "But we have to be in the top half of the table with all the Conference restructuring that will be going on."

"Do you think you'll be involved?" I asked.

"Well we have the ground and the money; we just need a few more Premier Division quality players in the team". He pointed out the seats behind one of the goals. "This summer we have a grant to put a roof on those." He paused. "It's not bad considering we were in the Northern Counties East League a year or so ago, and now we have won our biggest ever league title."

I wandered out to await the start of the match, but had to make a run for the stand on the far side of the ground, past the uncovered seating, as the heavens reopened. It is the sort of shower that brings to mind camping and cricket, the short sharp summer shower. As I reached the stand the noise on the roof was almost deafening. This made the tannoy almost unintelligible but I'm pleased to say that a kind Alfreton fan had the line-ups and showed me his programme. Just as the teams kicked off the shower subsided.

Alfreton as you would expect began stronger. The highly rated Ryan France, who may or may not be sent to Coventry during the summer in return for a suitable fee, played a lovely one-two with Goddard but put the ball wide with just a couple of minutes on the clock. Sports put pressure on themselves when Sutton fouled Askey on the right wing. Dolby swung in the resulting free kick and Hobson was unchallenged to meet it a couple of yards out. Wilson got a touch to it but couldn't keep it out.

If Alfreton didn't feel able to play free flowing football now they never would, and they looked likely to increase their lead. France headed just over and Goddard fired straight at Wilson. When another free kick was headed clear by the Mickleover defence John Knapper was there to volley it in from outside the penalty box for a magnificent goal.

As much as blue shirted Mickleover tried they couldn't test Ross Turner in the Reds goal. They got possession a few times but the crosses either drifted out for goal kicks or were simple catching practice. Eventually they managed to cause Alfreton problems when Parkins forced his way to the goalline and fired a shot past Turner and across the goal but there was no one to finish. The Reds responded by going to the other end and forcing Wilson into two good saves.

Since the first leg Mickleover had clinched the title and the Wilkinson Sword Trophy, which was strangely enough, a sword. This could be a double edged sword, if you pardon the pun, since the winning captain could be arrested for carrying an offensive weapon as soon as he is presented with it. They beat Pontefract Colliery over two legs in that duel. Their defence parried the Yorkshiremen's attacks, and they reposted with goals from Karl Payne and Dean Smith to foil their opponents and win 3-1. I used to do fencing a few years ago but I can't think of many more puns.

Home fans around me were getting into a discussion over their side's future. One lady had been to Scarborough F.C. recently. "We will never get to that standard", she told the others. "Their ground is far better and they get much better gates. Do you really think we could maintain a club of that size?" I doubt Scarborough has regularly been held up as a model of success but everything is relative.

"I don't even think our gates will go up next season", my next seat neighbour added.

"If we ever got into the Conference we would never survive", a third person agreed. I was surprised by this realism. I know that Boro fans are infected with pessimism but football fans are usually renowned for their incredible optimism. Whilst there are teams that have risen dramatically, Wimbledon being the best example, clubs can usually only grow a finite amount. Neighbours Ilkeston had tried to live the dream over the past few seasons with their chairman helping to fund a comparatively large playing budget in order to try and crack the Conference. Despite a good team they never averaged more than 700 which was not enough to break even. Now that budget was being cut and they found themselves spiralling down.

Whilst this discussion was carrying on Chris Parkins, one of four former Reds in the Sports side, almost grabbed a goal. He knocked the ball over the advancing Turner, only to see the ball cleared off the line by a last ditch clearance from ex-Chesterfield full back Mark Jules.

At half time I wandered over to the snack bar for a cup of tea. "Do you want milk with that, duck", the girl asked me. I was beginning to get used to people calling me duck after two years residence in Derbyshire. For whatever reason it didn't take too long for me to accept older people

134

using the terms, but when people my age called me it I still paused.

I'm all in favour of local dialects though. Every so often I came across a phrase that was obviously a Derbyshireism. My first Christmas here I was told about the annual work's fuddle. When I asked what one was the rest of the staff looked at me strange as if I was a little slow, so nothing new there, and were surprised that I should think it was just a local expression. As far as they were concerned it was a universal expression for a party. I spent the next few days desperately asking non Derbyshire friends whether they knew what one was, and was reassured that they didn't know either so I didn't feel quite so silly. Still, I've not found out what "Black over Bill's mother's" means yet.

The second half was not the greatest football I've ever seen and was a bit of an anti-climax. Generally there were a lot of long balls as players struggled to raise themselves for anything after a long season. Alfreton again had the best chances, but there was lack of urgency and on one occasion midfielder Steve Circuit just tried to walk the ball into the back of the net. Their tempo did go up a bit when Mick Godber came on and desperately tried to get on the scoresheet, but most shots still lacked conviction.

Mickleover had a few chances to get a consolation goal. There was still opportunity for Ross Mays to show us his trademark backheel again. Controversy of sorts came when Parkins chased a through ball with Turner. The goalie looked to have handled the ball outside the area, but the referee thought he blocked it with his body. Of course when Mickleover actually put the ball in the net it was ruled out for offside.

Mickleover fans hadn't given up and got irate when they were penalised on the edge of the Alfreton penalty with ten minutes remaining, giving the referee a piece of their mind. "What are they getting so worked up about?" one Red fan behind me wondered.

"Well if they had scored it could have been the turning point of the match!" my next seat neighbour said to a chorus of laughs.

However it was Sports fans who were laughing four minutes later after skipper Cunningham passed to Karl Yeoman inside the penalty area. Yeoman turned and blasted the ball, which despite Turner getting part of his body behind it trickled into the net. Yes, Mickleover had actually scored.

The end of season nature of the game was brought home as a few people left early. "See you next season", one man called out to his friends.

"Have a good summer", another replied. The close season always seemed to come suddenly.

When the full time whistle went I walked round to see the presentation. Only half of the 172 crowd had remained to see the Cup lifted high. A presentation was also made to John Knapper as Supporters Player of the Year, and a player who had probably been in running for man of the match tonight. It was a popular choice with the fans, not surprisingly I suppose, considering most of them must have voted for him. From the chants they sang to him it seems part of his appeal is in the fact that he had rejected Ilkeston to play for Alfreton

Well, that was it. Eight months after seeing Alfreton beat Farsley Celtic I had finished my season of Derbyshire football with them beating Mickleover. Now what would I do for the next few months?

Alfreton Town 2 – 1 Mickleover Sports

Hobson 6   Yeoman 81

Knapper 25

136

Alfreton win 7-1 on aggregate

Alfreton: Turner, Bradshaw, Jules (Highfield 77), Hobson, Heath, Knapper, France, Circuit (Johnson 71), Goddard, Askey (Godber 64), Dolby

Mickleover: Wilson, Warren, Mays, Yeoman, K. Reynolds, Sutton, Payne, Stevens, Parkins, Cunningham, Cliff subs not used: Wraith, Wedd, P. Reynolds

Attendance: 172

There were only a few clubs whose seasons went down to the wire. Mickleover had nearly been joined by Shirebrook in gaining promotion to the Premier Division. However their portakabin dressing rooms were not acceptable to the higher division so Borrowash were safe for another year.

Glossop North End and Chesterfield both escaped relegation by the skin of their teeth. Glossop, who'd had a decent run in, were left sweating as the teams below them still had games to play but results went the way of the Hillmen and they were safe. Chesterfield, who were now without Rushbury who had resigned, gave their fans a scare. They drew with Blackpool which was enough, although they missed a late penalty that would have made it more comfortable. The Spirites then announced former Ram Roy McFarland as new manager, whilst Rushbury became Director of Football at Alfreton.

Graham Streets Prims finished near the bottom but would not be relegated. Ilkeston Town knew their future well before the end of the season too. With rumours abounding that the chairman and managing director would be quitting, their league placing was the least of their worries. Although the future without the man who gave £250,000 a year to the club was worrying, some supporters hoped that this would galvanise the club and get more fans involved.

Belper would have qualified for the play-offs with a last day win, but they were playing at local rivals Matlock who naturally did them no favours by holding them to a draw.

Derby County had been safe for a while, but once the season was completed it was confirmed that John Gregory was to be sacked. Still with massive debts it looked like a close season to forget for Derby fans.

The Hudson Awards

This was the time of year when players and officials dug out their best suits and headed off to posh hotels for the annual awards dinners. Here they could celebrate their achievements or drown their sorrows and look forward to brighter days next season. Use your imagination then to picture such an event in a plush hotel. Since it is imaginary it can be as swanky as you like. Representatives from all the county clubs are here for a fun evening, and there are a number of trophies awaiting distribution. Here are my awards.

Website of the Season

I had spent much of the season online browsing the websites of the clubs featured in this book. Ilkeston managed to boast three, although the official website contained little topical information and the *Ilson Online* site folded weeks before the end of the season because the webmaster didn't have enough time to keep it updated. Updating it every Saturday evening and during the week must be an enormous commitment and another job that usually goes unnoticed.

Most of the websites were impressive. Buxton, Alfreton and Glossop all impressed, but Gresley Rovers win my hypothetical award. An impressive home page briefly listed the latest news and the latest webforum topics, whilst giving details of the last and next fixtures, and the league table. Other features included a database of all the players who had played for the Moatmen in the last 50 or so years. What really stood out though was, as I mentioned previously, the latest score feature that was updated within seconds of a goal. I'm tempted to say that technology has gone too far when anyone in the world can find out up to the minute scores from Church Gresley, but then again I take this facility for granted for the Boro.

Programme of the Season

As a programme connoisseur I eagerly read programmes at each match. Many were very good. Ilkeston and Alfreton in particular had excellent programmes. Ilkeston's had a lot of information about themselves as well as the visitors, including photos. They also had some good features and articles. I'm afraid though they were pipped by Derby County, who I suppose are at an advantage with a full time media department to compile it.

Goals of the Season

Being controversial I am only including goals scored by Derbyshire teams. In all but the odd occasion I'm just reliant upon my eyesight and memory, but at least that means few people can argue with me.

No.5   Steve Johnson
Long Eaton United v Shirebrook Town
Not particularly spectacular, but a good example of a careful build up. Shirebrook patiently passed the ball around the edge of the penalty area before spotting an opening. Johnson ran onto a good pass that split the defence and he casually slotted home the ball.

No.4   Aaron O'Connor
Ilkeston Town v Worcester City
A goal he created himself, since he had to dispossess a Worcester defender. After this he dribbled past two players before sending the goalkeeper the wrong way to score.

No.3   John Knapper
Alfreton Town v Mickleover Sports
A beautiful volley from outside the penalty box after a free kick was headed away. A real 'screamer'.

No.2   Steve Taylor
Matlock Town v Bishop Auckland

He received the ball just inside the Bishops half. He dribbled all the way to the penalty box, shrugging off defenders' challenges and then fired the ball past the advancing goalie into the bottom left hand corner of the net.

No.1   Leigh Grant
Graham Street Prims v Greenwood Meadows
An audacious backheel found Grant with his back to goal on the edge of the box. He turned, beat three players and smashed it into the back of the net. It was move that would have been raved about had it have been shown on TV. Well, none were there at The Asterdale that day so you'll have to take my word for it.

Team of the Season

Mickleover won their title and the Wilkinson Sword, although I didn't see them win any of the three games I saw. Glossop deserve credit for the way they battled back from two goals down after just ten minutes to draw against a strong Mossley side. Ilkeston were in a rich vein of form when I finally saw them, and seeing them from the Clock Tower stand made it memorable.

Team of the Year in my awards must go to Alfreton Town though. They led the table for most of the year, having a good FA Trophy run before winning the Derbyshire Senior Cup comfortably. And to think some supporters were disappointed with the season...

Match of the Season

I enjoyed most matches I attended, but some stood out more than others. Graham Street Prims v Greenwood was a nine goal thriller, which went right down to the wire. Ilkeston's game was good too, with a few strange incidents that always make a match stand out. I had a good day out at Buxton, and the Glossop North End game was well worth the £3 entrance fee. The first leg of the Derbyshire Senior Cup saw two teams in great form.

My vote and hypothetical trophy must go to Long Eaton United v Shirebrook. Only a couple of goals but it was a great game. Shirebrook were the stronger team but Long Eaton were always in with a shout and both team played good football.

Postscript:

Belper Town v Boston Town
Christchurch Meadows
FA Cup Preliminary Round
Saturday 30th August 2003

This match is a little late. You see I should have seen Belper play Farsley Celtic at the start of May in their last home match of the season. I thought it would be a good match to end my season with, but the week before I had a shock when I read that Belper's season had already ended with their draw at Matlock. Belper's website had disappeared into the great recycle-bin in the sky during the season so I had relied on the fixtures issued in August. Sometime during the year the Northern Premier League had obviously decided to end a week earlier. Therefore my visit was delayed till the 2003/04 season.

I had to include Belper in my travels, partly because the football club is one of the top non-league sides in the county, but also because it gave me an excuse to revisit the town. Belper is a historic town in the Derwent Valley, just a few miles south of Matlock and ten miles north of Derby. Their nickname, the Nailers, comes from the traditional industry of the area, nail making. The first mention is in 1250 but it is likely to have been begun soon after the Norman Conquest. The town got a reputation for producing quality nails, and it is said that Cowboys over in America used Belper nails.

The Nailers is quite a macho name, so it is no surprise that the club chose this over the other famous local industry, hosiery and stocking making. The Stockings doesn't have quite the same ring. However after the introduction of the hosiery industry to Belper in 1776 by Jedediah Strutt it soon became the dominant industry.

The mills along the Derwent played an important part in Britain's history, being amongst the first factories in the country and employing ground-breaking practices. In recognition of this a stretch of the Derwent from Cromford down to Derby has been made a World Heritage Site by the United Nations. Since their ground, Christchurch Meadows, is next to the Derwent, Belper is probably one of the only football clubs in the world to be inside a World Heritage Site. Not a bad boast compared to some clubs' claims to fame.

As I came up the A6 I wondered what sort of match I would be in for. Belper had been one of the front runners last season, behind Alfreton, but faded towards the end as their rivals won games in hand and overtook them to deny them a play-off place by a point or two. This season they had won both home games and lost both away games. Around this time it is hard to know what to expect, since you never know what performance is going to be typical, and which is a rare off day, or even a rare on day.

The sun shone brightly as I got off the bus, and since I had plenty of time I wandered around the town, ignoring the attraction of a 'Genuine quality hand wash'. On closer inspection of the small print it seems it was only cars they did. I spent a while looking at the cottages built by the paternalistic Strutts who constructed houses to accommodate their new workers and some of these cottages still exist virtually opposite Christchurch Meadows. It is an amazing sight to see this long street, suitably called Long Row, of cottages that could be in an open-air museum. Houses which were built to house the downtrodden workforce are now desirable residences commanding hefty sums.

Christchurch Meadows itself is an interesting little ground. The actual ground was rather plain, with an unobtrusive main stand along one side, but it was surrounded by lovely views on all sides. On one side you could see the other side of the valley, to the North the giant East Mill towered over the ground, whilst behind one goal stood Christchurch, hence the name of the ground.

Today's facilities must be considered a luxury by former Belper players. During the early days (cue Hovis music) the players had to change in a hotel a quarter of a mile away on the other side of the Derwent. I wonder if any visiting teams got lost on their way! After a while the club found a better solution, they bought old pig and fowl pens for the players to change in. Things could have been worse though because for a time it looked as though Christchurch Meadows would be bulldozed by a planned road, until they went to see the Minister of Transport to change his mind. All I have to go on is that phrase in a book, but my imagination conjures up certain pictures. I imagine a whole load of angry footballers and committeemen storming Whitehall and invading the Minister's office and demanding action or else. I'm sure the reality is far more boring.

If the match conditions were perfect, the match wasn't. The game never really got going, with both sides struggling to put moves together. Belper's midfield struggled with the basics of passing and ball control as they found it hard to create anything. It might have been different if the Nailers had converted an early chance. A ball from the right wing was headed back across the goal by skipper Steve Kennedy but Marc Ward, just four yards out had to juggle with the ball to try and get a clear shot in but in the end flicked it wide.

The home supporters were getting frustrated as their side failed to show the division in class between the sides. One man muttered that Belper had dropped to Boston's level. At least the defence seemed confident. Joey Winston, moderator of the unofficial Belper Message Board, had told me that apart from the impressive Ward, defenders Crookes and Jones were players to look out for. More than once they amazed me by nonchalantly passing the ball

145

around in their own box with Boston strikers around them. Although impressive I thought it also showed a lack of urgency.

Belper, in their yellow shirts, had a couple of chances, but they were weak shots that never really threatened. Drama was about to come though. As Belper cleared a cross for a corner Dean Jones got into a tangle with an opponent. Both players saw red and started pushing and shoving each other. The referee took a lenient view and just warned the antagonists. Minutes later Liam Walshe got involved in a similar incident and also escaped with a lecture.

Six minutes before the break a ball ricocheted to Boston's Price after Belper thought they had cleared an attack. Price was in acres of space on the left of the penalty area and he blasted the ball in off the far post for the first goal. It was very well taken and not undeserved. "This is what the FA Cup's about", I heard someone behind me say through gritted teeth, "meeting a bigger team on an off day and beating them." There were still 50 minutes to go but Belper would have to improve markedly. Strikers Ward and Evans seemed to be on different wavelengths and struggled to pass to each other, and too often they were alone up front without support from midfield.

At half time I chatted to the man behind me, Peter, about how he thought Belper would do this season. "Same as last year", he replied, "we'll struggle". This surprised me, since 6th in the table didn't strike me as struggling. "We'll be mid-table I suppose, or perhaps it will be a relegation struggle."

I asked him what the problem was. "The manager, Gary Marrow", was the simple reply. "We are too negative. One goal is enough for him, or two at the very most.

"He brought in a lot of players from Yorkshire on decent money but unfortunately many didn't work out and left. So what we are left with is a disjointed side." The substitutes

146

had been having a kick around during the interval but they were now heading back to the tunnel. "A couple of these, Simpson and Turner, are very talented", Peter told me, "but for some reason they are not getting a game." As an outsider I was unable to comment, but I have yet to meet a football fan anywhere, myself included, who didn't think they knew more about football than the manager.

It was also a surprise because Belper, unlike some other local teams, were at a high point in their short history. Until 1997 they had only played in the Central Alliance League, Midland League and Northern Counties East Leagues. Although they won each title, on one occasion with the help of Kevin Hector's goals, they had to wait before their ground was approved before making their move up to the Northern Premier League. Recent years had also brought an FA Vase semi-final and twice they had fallen just short of an FA Cup first round appearance, a feat they didn't look like repeating today.

The Nailers were stronger in the second half, although that wasn't saying much. Boston seemed to be prepared to hang on to the one goal lead. "Slow it down", was frequent call from their captain. Throw-ins, corners and free kicks were happily conceded as they broke up Belper's forays forward. It meant that Belper had considerable possession, if only they could use it.

Some of the free kicks brought chances, and they were unlucky when Kennedy narrowly failed to get on the end of a good cross by Liam Walshe and then Ward but put a shot wide. The next free kick was a bit strange though, when Walshe kicked the ball straight at the one-man wall. The player crumpled and the referee booked Walshe. Surely he hadn't intended hitting the ball into the wall instead of crossing in the hope of getting the important equaliser? Well if it was I think that is the first such yellow card I've seen.

Belper seemed to get more and more frustrated as the game progressed and their passes seemed rushed. Former Matlock midfielder Andy Simpson was brought on, and later Turner came on too. "Too late", Peter called out in frustration. They both looked good, but time was running out and the Boston defence looked unbreachable.

The closing minutes saw a number of chances, as firstly Ward went down in the area, but the referee said play on. Then the same player went on a run with the ball round the edge of area without finding a way past the defenders. A great cross then found Simpson a few yards out but his header looped onto the top netting.

"Oh well, we can concentrate on the league", someone muttered, but it was not all over. Two minutes into injury time the lively Ward found himself in space on the left. He cut inside and produced a great cross for Sean Gummer to head home from point blank range. The Belper fans behind the goal went wild. It nearly got better as Belper came forward again and a panicky Boston defence struggled to clear their lines. The referee then brought proceedings to a halt and both sides celebrated still being in the cup.

It was not the greatest game for me to end my odyssey, but it did sum football up well. "I bet you won't be rushing back here", Peter said to me when I told him that I was just visiting today. At many of the clubs I'd visited I had been encouraged to come again after my quest was over and perhaps become a regular. Buxton and other Northern sides were probably a bit too far, but perhaps I would return to some of the clubs when I wasn't going to the Riverside. I think I was going to miss it.

Belper Town 1 – 1 Boston Town
Gummer 90   Price 39

Belper: Ingham, Carter (Turner 76), Stratford, Crookes, Kennedy, Jones, Butler (Simpson 53), Walshe, Evans

148

(Gummer 61), Ward, Allsop. Subs (not used) Wlkinson, Greaves.

Boston: Ward, Ruscillo, Brooks, Rippin, Pell, Don-Duncan, Lawrence (Mee), Barclay, Bell, Langford, Price. Subs (not used) Clayton, Vaughan, Brader, Basford.

Attendance: 208

Post post-script

On Tuesday night Belper managed to win 1-0 to progress to the first qualifying round and claim their £1,000 prize money. According to Joey Winston on his website Belper were still pretty poor and rarely looked like scoring. In fact they had to rely on an own goal following another Ward cross. At least the defence was said to have played well again. Of course this was against a team a division below them.

152